GEORGES BRAQUE

G.BRAQUE

BY MAURICE GIEURE

ÉDITIONS PIERRE TISNÉ - PARIS
UNIVERSE BOOKS, Inc., NEW YORK

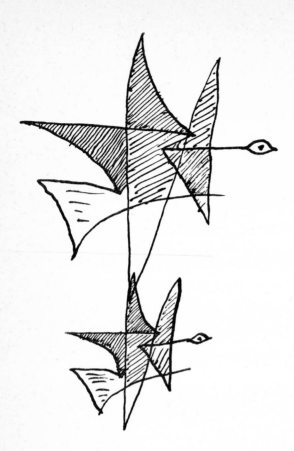

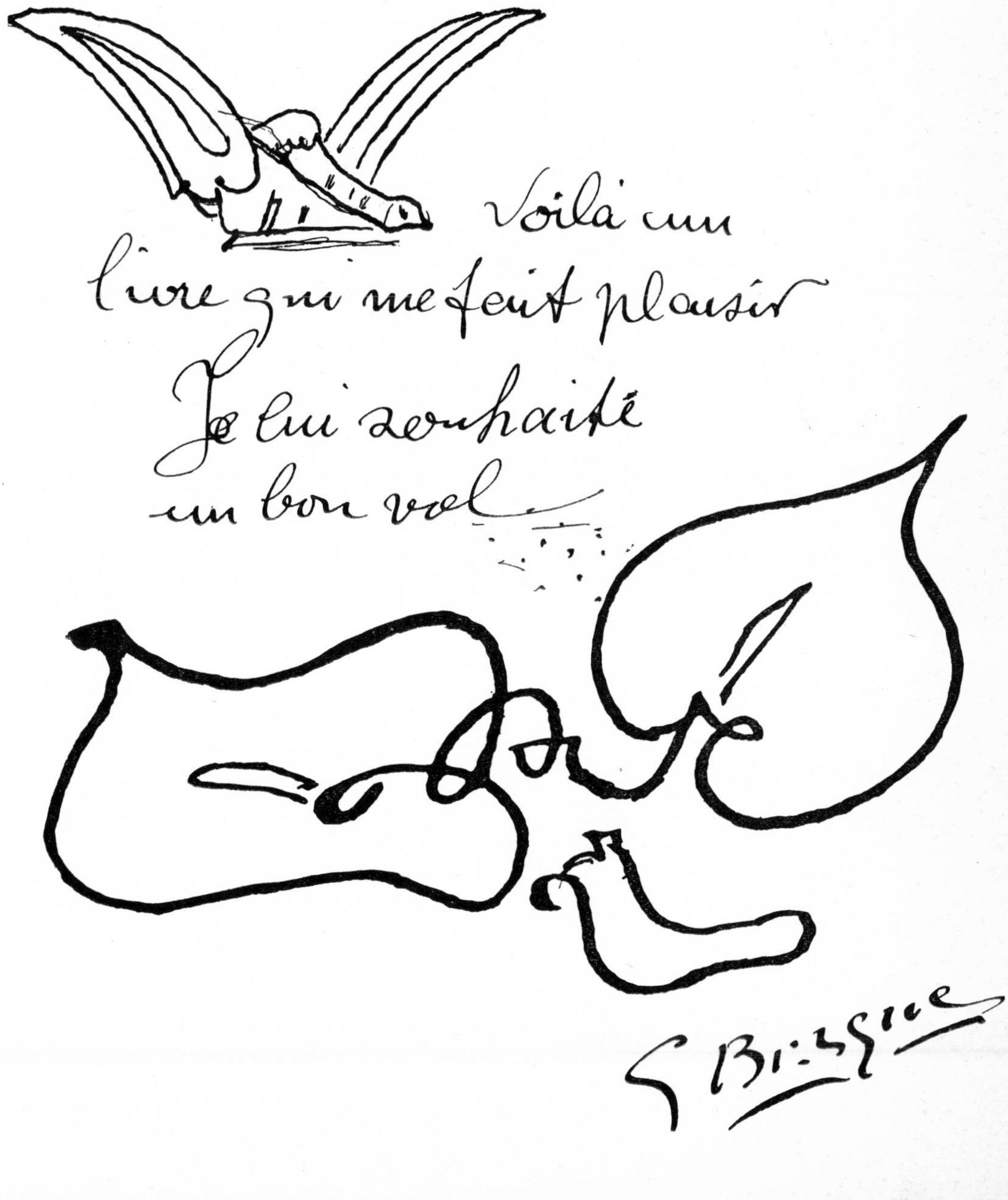

Voilà un
livre qui me fait plaisir
Je lui souhaite
un bon vol

G Braque

G Braque

HIS WORK AND ITS MEANING

THE name of Georges Braque must surely evoke in us not only the thought of his work but that of a whole lifetime dedicated to art. The fact that such pictures of his as spring to our minds, form an ordered succession of images, makes us realize that the work of this master-painter, for such he is, in spite of his modesty, has a striking continuity. Each picture is but a new and different state of what Braque calls the "pictorial fact", by which he means the picture considered as an entity in its own right apart from any story it may tell. Each picture, too, is a new realization of the picture space, whose constructive elements he has been investigating ever since his Fauve period.

His life has been a priesthood consecrated to his art and because of this he has succeeded more than any other painter in transposing himself into his works. He has summed up his achievement, in all its extraordinary density, in two phrases : "The painter thinks in form and color; his object is poetic creation." "The painter must not try to remake a story but to bring about a *pictorial fact*," and he says further: "One must not imitate what one wants to create... I want to put myself in unison with nature rather than to conjure it up... To discover a thing is to expose it to the quick... One must reach a certain temperature, which makes things malleable." And he points out the necessity of "impregnation, obsession and hallucination." All these taken together constitute the theory of *poetic creation* which is particularly his own and which is the key to the "pictorial fact" and the "unison with nature" to be found in all his pictures. One can only understand his painting by understanding the lyrical nature of its origin and completion and by participating in his won enthusiasm and exaltation.

Braque's conception of painting is "spiritual" to an astonishing degree. Every picture in its inception, continuation and completion is a lyrical problem as well as one for the painter's craft; it is an ideal or lyrical theme set out in the form of an ideogram. It is a question for him of making an "aesthetic object," the "pictorial fact," which will also be a "lyrical object" by its radiation or, if you like, its resonance. And therein lies the "poetic creation." "Art is a method of representation," he writes; "it is personal to the artist. The greater or the more inspired the artist, the more it will outstrip reality and achieve value as painting."

All his pictures must be considered on two levels, that of appearance and that of meaning. The level of appearance is the painted work with its plastic realities, color, line, form and rhythm, something concrete and sufficient unto itself. The level of meaning is reached of necessity by going beyond the appearance to the deep aesthetic and lyric values, that is from knowledge by seeing to knowledge by understanding. We enter in the abstract realm of symbols, separate from ordinary reality, which tend to become, and do become ideograms, signs to be studied until their meaning becomes clear.

"The painter thinks in form and color; his object is poetic creation." The level of appearance, with its forms and colors, figures forth and provides the level of meaning which depends on it for its existence, but it is not sufficient by itself when the signs of which it is composed are ideograms. It is sufficient in the works of Cézanne, Matisse or Dufy but not in those of Picasso and Braque. In these two cases an "aesthetic object" is created which becomes a "lyrical object" by its significance. Whatever their nature, the paintings are more or less abstract ideograms using reality as a pretext. For Cézanne, Matisse and Dufy, this reality is predominantly, though not exclusively, plastic. For Picasso and Braque, it is ideological as well. For all of them, the level of appearance is always a level of plastic significance, but whereas the three former painters are content to leave it as such, for Braque and Picasso it is also a medium to express poetic or lyrical meaning. Thus the level of plastic significance is the "aesthetic object" and the level of poetic meaning the "lyrical object."

The "aesthetic object" is the work as it exists physically and materially by its craftsmanship, independently of its meaning. A Bach fugue is a pure aesthetic object. It develops as a musical composition according to fixed rules and has no meaning beyond this development. It is not beautiful because it signifies something but because it is well constructed. If it gives certain hearers an extra-musical vision or emotion, it is a case of transferred susceptibility. And clearly if the theme is beautiful, the fugue will be even more so.

As a pure æsthetic object, a work of art can only be completely understood (which is quite different from being *felt*) by a technical knowledge of its formal organization and analysis of the figures constructing it. The structure of the forms and figures is constituted by the relations between them, consolidated into a whole by their interdependence.

A few examples will allow me to make my meaning clearer.

I - Goya's *Old Women*.—This is an æsthetic object if we consider only its composition, its chromatic relations, rhythms and interconnections and its construction with an ascending diagonal from right to left. The subject, Death mowing down two horrible old women, is not an absolute element in the composition as the picture could have been painted otherwise, with the same characters but with different rhythms, colors and construction, and still have the same meaning.

This meaning, by the emotive power of the images which give it form, is an addition to the æsthetic object containing it and makes of it a lyrical object. We pass from appearance to meaning. The lyrical quality was present in the idea of the work but it took a painter of genius, an inventor of form, to achieve the picture in a series of lyrical states, recalling, modifying and amplifying the original inspiration.

II - *The Wedding at Cana* by Veronese.—It is simply a banquet in Venice and the painting is no more than an æsthetic object. Its value, its beauty, its greatness (not of size but of prestige) lie entirely in the composition. If there is any lyrical quality, it is of form only. The most one can say is that its pomp, its grandeur, its magnificence, thoroughly Venetian and of the period, have a sort of lyricism of munificence, which does not, however, move one in the slightest.

III - *The Balcony* by Manet.—In this picture, the painter's chief object was to place three figures, two women and a man, in a general scheme of blacks, greys, with a few colors, white, and the green ironwork of a balcony in the foreground. Nothing lyrical, nothing to stir the emotion. The subject, three figures on a balcony, is no more than a theme for a painting, neither anecdotal nor poetic, nothing more than Goya's "Majas on the Balcony" which Manet had in mind. It is exclusively an "æsthetic object," a plastic composition. The only problem to solve was to secure the maximum tonal value by the placing of the figures and the quality and quantity of their color relations both among themselves and with the background. The figures are objects of the same order as the flower pot and its flowers, the dog, the shutters, the balustrade, the man's cravat, and what one can just see at the back of the room. They are part of an immobility whose only particular value is the color rhythm it forms in the total rhythm of the picture.

IV - *Cézanne's pictures* (after 1874, Cézanne in the flowering of his genius). Every picture by Cézanne is a pure æsthetic object. He was the first liberator of painting and freed it entirely from anecdote. What he wanted was to create on the two dimensions of the canvas, a "flow" of colored forms engendering both volume and light in a filled-up space.

A Cézanne picture is not beautiful because it is moving, it is lyrical in proportion to its beauty and the beauty results from the proportions of the composition.

A Greek temple is beautiful because its proportions are necessary and above all sufficient. The same may be said of a Gothic cathedral or a Romanesque church; they move us by the atmosphere which they impose, and their achievement is the creation of a spiritual emotion which is as fine as it is pure.

The work of Cézanne moves us because it is a continual power current by which we are affected. The emotion comes from the painting and from nothing but the painting. We are affected not by what he tells us but by what he has done. He does not create an unknown world, imaginary, fictitious or emotive, but a world in which every object is given its formal values and its spiritual values. Every picture is sufficient unto itself both in what it represents and in the spiritual region beyond the appearance. It is, in fact, a lyrical object, since for Cézanne, as for Braque, "the object is poetic creation."

"When what was at first a splash of white becomes a table-cloth, the plastic attains its poetic form". Braque is here more explicit, the painter thinks in forms and colors, in this case the splash of white, the symbol or ideogram; it turns into a table-cloth and the plastic becomes poetic.

The lyrical object and the æsthetic object are thus seen to be reversible to the extent that the former only exists through the latter and the latter is only present in order to turn into the former. But since the æsthetic must grow into the lyric, which is its final form, the aesthetic object, in view of its inner meaning, is bivalent, or even ambivalent; it is more than it appears to be. But the lyrical object is necessarily *monovalent*, being the final achievement, the sum total of the work and nothing else but that.

Let us take another picture by Goya: *Youth*, with its disturbing sensuality. The principal and most prominent figure is the young girl on the right, hand on hip, reading what is probably a love letter. What detail is it in her young beauty, which draws the eye? The white corsage on the bosom which can be divined under the gauze, almost naked and offered to us without any shame, by the transparent veil and the position of the thrust-forward body. The lyrical object consists of this sensuality, this barely disguised eroticism. It is the same with the *Maja desnuda* where the emphasis is on the full breasts, and with the *Painter's Mistress*, a half length figure with the coil of the mantilla framing the unveiled breasts which Goya loved. The true, the deep meaning of these pictures lies in the bosom; the rest is but the setting.

Take El Greco's paintings; the composition is no more than the presentation of a mystic theme of which the figures are so many ideograms. Or take Van Gogh, that other mystic painter. His pictures are always and entirely the hallucinating expression of his hallucinated soul. For him, as for Braque, it is a question of "*Impregnation-Obsession-Hallucination*."

Thus the lyrical object gives the work the meaning which consummates it spiritually. The craftsman which every artist must be, becomes a visionary.

Georges Braque is such a visionary, not a mystic like El Greco or Van Gogh, nor a misanthrope like Goya, nor an expressionist like Picasso, but an entirely spiritual painter, who transforms vulgar reality into poetic creation.

IMPREGNATION — THE FAUVE YEARS

IMPREGNATION — OBSESSION — HALLUCINATION. This last has been described by Braque as the definitive realization of a long impregnation beginning in his youth, an impregnation by things which struck him at a time when he was not fully conscious of them and subsequently pursued him until they became real. "A painting which does not *disturb* you, what good is it?"

He was born on May 13, 1882, at Argenteuil, near Paris, of a local family and is thus not a Norman as many believe. His paternal grandfather, his father Charles and his mother Augustine Johanet were all born at Argenteuil. Georges Braque and his family lived in his grandfather's house in the rue de l'Hôtel Dieu. The latter had a painting business; his son Charles assisted him and may perhaps be considered as a "Sunday painter"; he even showed at the *Salon des Artistes Français*. Braque himself drew from his earliest youth.

In 1890, when he was eight years old, the family moved to Le Havre, 33, rue Jules Lausne, and he took a keen interest in the life of the harbor which was to become familiar to him. At school he was a middling pupil, given to long bicycle rides, boating, bathing and sport in general. While still a schoolboy he enrolled in evening classes at the *Ecole des Beaux-Arts* under M. Courchet. He learned to draw with charcoal and stump from antique plaster models, as did Raoul Dufy and Othon Friesz at the same period under Thuillier. He was then allowed to work from life.

At seventeen he left school and his father, Charles, took him into his painting business and the same year, 1899, he was apprenticed to Roncy who had a similar business. At the *Ecole des Beaux-Arts* he painted in oils and began to paint in the country on Sundays. From this period date the *Portrait of his Grandmother* (Pl. 1), and that of his *Cousin Johanet* (Pl. 2), thoroughly academic pictures with chiaroscuro. At the Havre museum he often looked at two landscapes by Boudin, one by Corot and another by Toulouse-Lautrec, pictures which were also seen by Dufy and Friesz. The Impressionist School was unknown to him except through articles appearing in *Gil Blas*. In addition to painting, he added to his artistic education by going to the theater and learning to play the flute with Gaston Dufy, Raoul's brother, whom he had known since 1898. During the summer holidays at Honfleur he went out for bicycle expeditions during which he painted.

At the end of the year 1900 he came to Paris where he continued his apprenticeship as a painter and decorator with Laberthe. He rented a room in Montmartre and took the municipal art course at Les Batignolles, directed by Guignolot. This new apprenticeship as a painter-decorator perfected him in the craft and technique of reproducing imitation marble, rare woods, masonry and wall-paper, and also in the preparation and mixing of paints and the use of different grounds on which to paint. We may wonder whether he ever surmised the importance of this training in his work and the fact that a very large part of his personality as a painter and the character of his pictures, once the preliminaries of Fauvism, the Cézanne period and early Cubism were over, would be due to this "technical impregnation."

With what art, with what masterly composition, he was to use not only the shape of walls, their angles and their vertical and horizontal lines, but even more the wall-paper motifs which he introduced into the plastic rhythms of his pictures, and with what art he later made use of his painting "material," preparing canvases with the addition of sand and plaster and engraving vast figures on blackened plaster.

It was this continual preoccupation with his "raw material," with the specific value of tones and form, of concrete realities, which led him, from early Cubism on, to introduce lettering into the picture, to stick colored or printed paper onto the canvas, or to use gouache, charcoal, crayon, chalk and *papiers collés* in one and the same work, in order to obtain particular plastic effects.

The fact that he lived in the port of Le Havre, facing the sea, and knew the life of the harbor so intimately, has not, I think, a great importance in his work. If he has always been faithful to the sea, it is as a man rather than as a painter that he is affected by it. He has always loved the delightful coast between Havre and Dieppe and, as soon as he could, acquired a house at Varengeville where he spends his summers.

The sea has never meant for him the scene of joyful excitement and luxurious festivity that it was for Dufy, nor did it induce in him a Baudelairian spleen as in Marquet. The sea, for Braque, is the Channel seen at the bottom of the cliffs, on the shingles where the boats are beached. It is that which is no longer land but a mysterious immensity, devourer of men and dreams, the sea, terrible even in its calm.

Though he was to find the waterfront atmosphere again in Antwerp, in 1905 and 1906, and though he was tempted, for a short while, by the exciting Mediterranean color at L'Estaque and at La Ciotat, he never painted the sea again until much later, in a few pictures which are extraordinarily beautiful and often tragic. Braque does not paint the sea as a spectacle but as an element. "The painter should not try to make a story for himself," he says, and he puts himself "in unison" with the sea to express its cosmic grandeur and to draw from it a superb and menacing poetic creation.

In 1901 he was called up for military service and stationed near Le Havre, where he met Diéterle, a Paris picture dealer, and Albert Henraux, who had no idea of their companion's artistic merit. They considered him as a strapping six-foot fellow who sang the soldiers' songs better than anyone and loved to dance. At the end of a year's service he had been made sergeant.

Back in civilian life he returned to the capital, to the rue Lepic, and enrolled at the *Academie Humbert*, boulevard Rochechouart, where he met Picabia and Marie Laurencin. In the fall of 1902 he presented himself at the *École des Beaux-Arts*, and was admitted to the studio of Léon Bonnat, who had also accepted Othon Friesz and Raoul Dufy. But he, like Dufy, chafed under the servile academicism of that teacher and after two months returned to the *Académie Humbert*.

He spent the summer of 1904 at Honfleur where he found Raoul Dufy and made friends with the sculptor Manolo and the critic Maurice Raynal. There is a painting by him of this period in the Havre Museum: *View of the Park at Honfleur*, which gives no indication as yet of the work to come.

At the end of the year he took a studio in the rue d'Orsel, in front of the *Théâtre Montmartre*, and went frequently to the Louvre, where he was strongly attracted to archaic Greek and Egyptian art. Among the painters he admired Poussin for his order and arrangement, and even more the works of Corot. He knew the Impressionists through Durand-Ruel and Ambroise Vollard, his preference going to Renoir and after him to Monet, Sisley and Pissarro. He was deeply moved by Van Gogh and Seurat, who put him off Gauguin and Degas.

In the summer of 1905 he lived at Quimperlé and at Le Havre where he painted a *View of the Harbor* with a sailing ship at the pier, a picture of admirably solid technique (Pl. 3).

GEORGES BRAQUE DANS SON ATELIER — 1955

Photographie de Mariette Lachaud

PORTRAITS DE BRAQUE

This year 1905 has an important place in the history of painting; it is that of the "official" birth of Fauvism. The name "Fauve" or wild beast was coined by Louis Vauxcelles, who later baptized Cubism.

In the *Salon d'Automne* there were canvases of Marquet, Rouault, Vlaminck, Manguin and Friesz, and Matisse's *Luxe, Calme et Volupté*. Braque did not take part; his first public exhibition was in the spring of 1906 at the *Salon des Indépendants*, where he showed landscapes painted at Le Havre and two still lifes. None of the pictures were "Fauve."

In 1905 and 1906 he went to Antwerp to paint, with Friesz. They stayed in a boarding-house near the harbor and rented a studio on the banks of the Scheldt, from the balcony of which they overlooked the river. Braque became a "Fauve" by contact with Friesz but did not use violent colors. It is from this period that his originality dates.

In Paris, in September, he painted views of the Canal St. Martin, and when he had had enough of the city, he moved south in search of the vivid light and distinctive colors of the Mediterranean, settling at L'Estaque, though not because he was attracted by the work of Cézanne; the latter so far meant nothing to him. He lived at the Hotel Maurin for several months, painting the harbor, the hills and the houses. These pictures are violently colored and powerfully constructed. He returned to Paris in the spring of 1907 and sent several pictures to the *Salon des Indépendants*, including landscapes and a *Seated Nude seen from Behind* (Pl. 10), which looks like a Matisse. He was incorporated among the "Fauves."

At the beginning of May he left again for the south and went to La Ciotat where Friesz joined him for the summer. The works he painted there are similar to those done at L'Estaque where he stopped again before returning to Paris.

The paintings of that fall show a change of manner and noticeable similarities with Cézanne. The colors are less and less violent; dominant grays and browns appear. In October, Daniel Henry Kahnweiler who had just opened a gallery at 28, rue Vignon, paid him a visit. He already had pictures by Picasso, Derain, Vlaminck and Van Dongen, bought Braque's *View from the Hotel Mistral* and his *Viaduct with Three Arches*, and soon afterwards made a contract for his entire output.

What was Fauvism? First of all, a violent reaction against Impressionism, against the disappearance of space in favor of overall lighting, against careful analysis, which became arbitrary instead of constructive, because only occasionally practiced, and against the supplanting by a facile technique of the well-tried æsthetics of open-air painting. Cézanne had understood this well and, influenced by Pissarro, returned to a strong, solid and, in a way, rational form of construction.

The Fauves also considered it imperative to get back to a powerful and well-devised equilibrium by the use of individual tones for particular objects and to return to a plastic process that should not be subservient to the motif with all its dazzling diversity.

What counted for a Fauve was color, not simply in itself but for its value as a component. A picture was a construction not a reproduction, a series of plastic connections, not a story in paint, an organization of violent colors and not just something "pretty."

Of all the Fauve painters, the greatest are Matisse, Dufy, Derain, Vlaminck and occasionally Van Dongen, because they are *entirely* Fauve. Apart from them, almost on the border line, Braque was only a Fauve because it gave him a freedom of expression and the plastic elements necessary to his meditation on both the ideology and the craft of painting. What distinguishes a Braque "Fauve" painting from others is not the colors he uses but the great care he takes in fitting them into his composition. He liked reds and pinks, green, including emerald, mauves, a number of violets, among them a magnificent *cyclamen* and a few yellows, shaded as far as orange.

And perhaps it is to the Fauve period that he owes his search for the all-important "pictorial fact," since the Fauves were looking for this also, exclusively in color and rejecting line which became no longer constructive but only included as an unmarked frontier between adjacent colors. In Braque this chromatic violence is neither defiant nor revolutionary; it is simply an organized construction. He could say already at this period: "I am for the rule which corrects the emotion... Construction is the assembling of homogeneous elements... I am not a revolutionary painter."

A picture painted in Antwerp in 1906, now owned by Baron von der Heydt (in Switzerland), has a very simple subject: *View of the Port*. (Pl. 4 shows a close variant of it).

In the foreground is a wharf, with a floating landing stage on the left and a little steamer drawing up to it: beyond it the river and a departing tug-boat on the right. In the background is the opposite wharf, with a cargoboat tied up, and finally the town, with the cathedral in silhouette. It is all in large masses, without detail. The work is wonderfully balanced by its juxtaposition of colors.

The wharf in the foreground is in two tones: mounting patches of cyclamen, separated by pale blue and then a bright yellow wash. A thick black line defines the edge of the wharf and the river begins, multicolored in cyclamen, blue-violet and red. Beyond the little steamer (black with a red water-line, white poop and tank, light yellow funnel and bridge and poppy-colored masts) and the violet-black landing-stage with its sepia tank splashed with the same yellow as the wharf, and its three flags (red and white, black and yellow, red and violet haloed in pink) beyond these the river is in modulated greens. Under the black cargoboat with its blue funnel, are five dashes of pink (a softened cyclamen). The brown hull becomes violet by touches of cyclamen. The town is in a number of greens and almost white yellows, the roofs dark violet, amethyst or slate-blue. The mass of the cathedral is green. The sky above is almost incandescent in rose-pink in which appear pale blues and very soft greens.

Thus although the basic color composition is very simple, violets, greens, yellows and a few blues and reds, it offers a wonderful diversity. The principle of "variations" is already in operation and we find his effervescent coloring and his "charm" (in its true magical meaning). From this time on, he thought in forms and colors, the simultaneousness of form and color which was the fundamental principle of Fauvism.

Another point of interest in this picture is its planning; first of all the wharf in the foreground and the sky and town above are two horizontal strips of the same width, which is half that of the horizontal strip of river; secondly the construction is entirely "woven" in horizontal and vertical lines. In fact, Braque's dearest principles are already in evidence.

In this picture and its variants and in all those of the same period, the painter's personality appears. What he took from the Fauves has been adapted to his own way of thought. The arrangement of the colors, the "weaving" of the structure, the planning of the "variations" constitute clearly the first stage of what was to be the unremitting pursuit of poetic creation, the achievement of a "pictorial fact" inserted in truly pictorial space. The variants of the picture are less subtle in coloring. In that of 1905, the *Port of Antwerp*, which is in the Kunstmuseum in Basel, the Impressionist or neo-Impressionist influence (that of Seurat) is clear. The little steamer has flags flying, the cargo boat is replaced by a white sailing ship also beflagged, the houses in the town are more precisely indicated, the mass of the cathedral is mauve. All the tones are more moderate (Pl. 8). In another variant, also of 1905, the cargo boat is white and the town looks the same as it does in the Basel picture.

What had happened between these two paintings of 1905 and that of the von der Heydt collection (1906) was that Fauvism had replaced Impressionism.

Braque was a Fauve in the same way that Renoir was an Impressionist, that is to say, for a short period only. He used Fauvism to discover himself as Renoir used Impressionism to enrich his art, and they both abandoned these respective schools when they began to realize themselves fully. The same can be said of Van Gogh, Cézanne and Gauguin, who though they were influenced by the kind of painting in which color is dominated by light never entirely adopted its technique and abandoned its æsthetic principles as soon as they could create what they themselves wanted.

Neither the Fauve technique nor its æsthetic principles gave Braque the real solution to his problem; they lacked a sufficiently strict discipline.

What he was to become was brought about by the revelation of Cézanne.

THE DISCOVERY OF CÉZANNE

THE discovery was not an immediate one. The spirit came before the letter in his impregnation by the works of the Aix master; he had to pass through pre-Cubism and the successive stages of Cubism from 1910 to 1914 until he became obsessed by Cézanne to the point of hallucination and the pictorial fact, poetic creation and finally pictorial space appeared to him attainable by successive developments of his art.

Fauve painting disappeared after 1907 and we may ask what the real reasons were for its disappearance.

Fauvism, far from being a discipline, was the almost anarchical exaltation of the personality of each painter. It was a question for each of them not only of outdoing the others but of surpassing his own accomplishment. The effort led to a sort of paroxysmal academicism, which was unnecessary and consequently disappeared. Its contribution to art, however, was far too valuable for it to be considered as a movement of no consequence.

The second reason why the Fauve painters abandoned Fauvism was their deeper knowledge of the work of Paul Cézanne whose influence replaced that of Gauguin and concealed Van Gogh's influence behind the regained architectural value of their pictures. This was true of France; in Germany, with *Die Brücke*, Expressionism came to life in the wake of Cézanne, or we should perhaps say, was reincarnated, as it is a fundamental element of the Germanic and Nordic soul.

In Braque's Fauve period we can already trace the influence, if not of Cézanne, at least of the latter's spatial and objective research and it was inevitable that the full influence should be felt sooner or later.

Braque began to realize more and more what he wanted. He was working toward the autonomy of the picture and Fauvism had suggested to him what it might be: a pure chromatic and plastic construction. He was also absorbed by another problem, that of the picture space, the synthesis of three dimensions on a two-dimensional plane.

Only a different æsthetic system and a different technique from Fauvism could help him to the first solutions of these two fundamental problems. The discovery of Cézanne, followed by the analytical study of his paintings, changed Braque's work without being the true cause of the change; that discovery was responsible for the crystallization or, if you like, it was the necessary catalyzing agent.

Cézanne had taken the problem of painting back to its very beginnings. He proposed a "conceptualism" of painting which, in its æsthetics and its execution, depended entirely on the "pictorial fact," that is to say, colored, volumetric representation. For him the motif was constructed spatially by successive perspective parallels in the direction of the horizon. The lines from the foreground to the background indicated the depth. Braque's visual space which "separates objects from each other," probably derives from this. In the still lifes, the space is filled up by the rhythmic juxtaposition of the volumes and light-color composed by the objects. This was the starting point for what was later to be Braque's tactile space "which separates us from the objects."

It was perhaps Cézanne's "Gardanne" period and the vertical construction of the town, which first affected Braque deeply. We soon find it carried to its extreme point, the reduction of depth to the two-dimensional plane of the canvas. Cézanne's "Gardanne" paintings and his last works in polyhedrons and even in "cubes," with a preponderantly blue-green lighting, in fact the overall atmosphere of Provençal "blue" as he always saw it in which the tones of individual objects are only indicated in light and color as part of the whole, these incited Braque to reduce his palette to the single tones which he found sufficient to express the construction and the juxtaposition of objects in the landscapes which he was now to paint.

Cézanne's influence was essentially deeper on Braque than on Picasso. The Spanish painter found in it a means of expressing himself but for Braque it was an end and an æsthetic system. He felt that by it, and only by it, he could achieve the "pictorial fact" and "pictorial space," by refashioning a world of objects without apparent connection into a visual *continuum*, so that all the figurative elements visually separated should become an organic whole, plastically connected by juxtaposition in the painting. He went further than Cézanne in a rhythmic condensation of space by which it lost perspective and came nearer and nearer to the level of the canvas until it was part of it. He went further still in true Cubism (analytic and synthetic) by inverting perspective and making objects appear to come out toward the spectator instead of being arranged in deliberate, artificial depth according to Italian perspective or such partial, undirected substitutes for it as we find in the Impressionists, Gauguin, Van Gogh and Cézanne.

It should not be thought that Braque at this period (1907-1909) had found a final solution; I want simply to show that he had increased the possibilities offered by Cézanne and that by far from haphazard intuition and deduction he was developing the essential elements of a solution, that is to say, the spatial and volumetric construction of a picture.

Space was no longer a series of juxtaposed realities within limited dimensions but the welding together of forms in a dense mass. The reality, motif and pretext of the work, developed as a whole without any apparent division. The painted work differed from observed reality by being made up of volumetric rhythms. Space was no longer an element of separation but a constructive element of liaison. It was used in the picture not to make a likeness but an equivalence; it did not distinguish objects individually in a sham perspective but accumulated one on top of another in an unseparated total. What was at a distance went on top and what was near became the bottom. Between top and bottom, by superposition, was the appearance of perspective. He returned to the simultaneous portrayal of the "Primitives," particularly those whose astonishing frescoes are to be seen in the Chapter House of Le Puy cathedral. He was not acting in imitation but according to an æsthetic system of superposing images on a surface—that of the canvas. Space was no longer an addition to representation but a plastic element of a certain rhythm in the composition, introduced by geometric volumes. Cubism was born, if not in its full realization, at least in its deep values, since in this geometrical treatment of volume, which carried Cézanne's work to its extreme conclusions, cubes were first chosen for their formal simplicity and the clarity with which they could be superimposed. Matisse was not wrong when he saw the *Houses at Estaque* (Pl. 12) and talked about "little cubes" (though he denied this later), and neither was Louis Vauxcelles.

Much has been written and said to the effect that Braque, when he saw Picasso's *Demoiselles d'Avignon* in 1907, which is an evocation of a certain Barcelona brothel, was inspired by the work to a presentiment of Cubism, though for Picasso Cubism came later, after his Negro period. The argument adduced in support of this is a Braque *Nude* of 1907 (Pl. 11). The influence of the *Demoiselles* on the *Nude* is undeniable, but I cannot see that it was really so important, as Braque was looking for something else.

Les Demoiselles d'Avignon has nothing in common with El Greco or Cézanne. The former's influence must be sought elsewhere, in the "evocation" of the Blue Period, and the latter's not until 1909 in the Horta period, which is very close to that of Cézanne's Gardanne pictures.

18

BRAQUE 1928

BRAQUE 1908

PICASSO 1908

BRAQUE 1925

VISAGES DE FEMMES

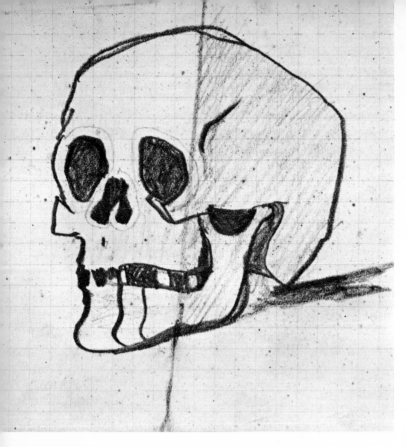

BARTHEL BRUYN (1524)

FLEURS ET CRANES

PICASSO (1945)

ALBERT DURER

By 1907 Picasso's Rose Period was over. He and Derain became acquainted, through Matisse at first, with Negro and Polynesian masks and primitive sculpture and *Les Demoiselles d'Avignon* is a combination of the Rose Period and the first Negro influence. One can see already the structural outline of the Negro Period. The three women on the left are painted in a monochrome flesh tint, reminiscent of the Rose Period but their forms are violently modeled with drawn-out lines. The two women on the right are highly colored and painted in places with parallel strokes, their forms following the direction of these strokes, the opposite to that indicated by the women on the left. The faces are a first sketch of the figuration in the Negro Priod. The work is undoubtedly a preparation for the Cubism to come, but at a distance and as yet ill-defined.

In the spring of 1908 Braque returned to L'Estaque with Raoul Dufy, whom he greatly influenced. The landscapes he did there are brilliantly original.

He gave up the Fauve coloring, put aside reds, blues and violets and limited himself to ochres, light greens and gray. The composition tightens up the structural lines by simplifying the masses into angular figures. The details of the landscape become a synthetic, global construction of elements chosen entirely for their figurative values and juxtaposed in a vertical order or succession.

It is here that he takes leave of Cézanne and goes beyond him. Cézanne's formal reduction of nature to the sphere, the cone and the cylinder—in Braque it is the cube—has, as a consequence, the transposition of what is seen into what is painted. The motif has become a pretext; the object is already poetic creation.

In this same year of 1908 at L'Estaque, Braque, in his still lifes, used musical instruments for theme and subject, among them the mandolin, which was the first appearance of what the guitar was to become in Cubism.

Why did he introduce this mandolin and this guitar into his painting? Because he was a musician? It is quite probable. We know that he learned to play the flute with Gaston Dufy and the names of Bach and Debussy can be found in his paintings. In the *Still Life* (Pl. 19) with musical instruments, which is still in his possession, we note, as well as a mandolin, a clarinet, an accordion and the open score which appears so often in his works. I think that to his taste for music there was added the plastic possibilities of the forms, the volumes offered by the mandolin, the guitar and the score. We shall see later that these instruments and the score, with their curves and angles, were full of formal possibilities for his work.

In the fall of 1907, through D.H. Kahnweiler, Braque got to know Picasso, who had been living since 1904 at 13, rue Ravignan with Max Jacob and Juan Gris, and he discovered the *Demoiselles d'Avignon*. The group known as that of the "Bateau-lavoir" was formed there, which included, as well as Picasso and Juan Gris, Metzinger, Marie Laurencin, Apollinaire, Max Jacob, André Salmon, Maurice Raynal, Princet, Gertrude and Leo Stein, and Kahnweiler.

From October 1st to the 22nd, 1907, in the 5th *Salon d'Automne* there was a retrospective Cézanne exhibition, including fifty-six works. His letters to Emile Bernard were published in which we find the following: "*Let me repeat to you what I was saying about the treatment of nature by the cylinder, the sphere and the cone, all in perspective...*", and again: "Lines parallel with the horizon give breadth, according to a natural reaction. Lines perpendicular to the horizon give depth. Nature, for us humans, is more in depth than on the surface..."

It can be well understood that the exhibition and the observations in this letter incited the Fauve painters to examine Cézanne's work closely.

At the 24th *Salon des Indépendants* (March 20-May 21, 1908), Braque showed three paintings and a drawing. In the summer he was at l'Estaque where he painted landscapes and a few still lifes, including the one with the musical instruments.

In September the jury of the 6th *Salon d'Automne* refused five out of the seven pictures he submitted and he withdrew the whole lot. It was then that Matisse, a member of the committee, is said to have spoken of "little cubes" in connection with the *Houses at L'Estaque*.

From November 9th to 28th he showed for the first time at the Kahnweiler Gallery, with Apollinaire writing a preface to the catalogue, and it was on this occasion that Louis Vauxcelles, the baptiser of schools, wrote in *Gil Blas* on November 14th: "Braque despises form and reduces everything, landscapes, figures and houses to geometric patterns, in fact to cubes."

In 1909 (March 25 to May 12) in the *Salon des Indépendants*, Braque, who did not show again with the group until 1920, had a *Landscape* and a *Still Life*, and Louis Vauxcelles wrote again, in *Gil Blas* of May 25th, about "cubist eccentricities." The name was born.

In summing up this admirable period of Braque's work, we should note, on the one hand, the exclusive value of his plastic composition, and on the other his discovery of a "filled space" which was the first approximation of a "pictorial space"; both in his still lifes and in his landscapes, plenitude was always attained. The distinction between visual space (which separates objects) and tactile space (which separates us from the objects) was not yet realized. Braque had discovered a kind of "pictorial space" and a wonderful plastic composition which did not yet comprise the integral reduction of the third dimension, that of depth, into the two others, but their superposition in a sort of representative equivalence of all three. Cubism was no longer a possibility only, it was a reality. A picture had an autonomous value as a painting, the visual motif was transmuted into a "pictorial fact" and the subject was no longer a motif but a pretext for an æsthetic disposition and organization. What Cézanne had begun, Braque had brought to fulfillment. The artist no longer aimed at a true representation but at a "total" picture.

A picture is a work which obeys the particular imperatives and essentials of painting; it is a rhythmic if not colored representation on a two-dimensional surface of realities which have three dimensions in nature. Others besides himself, Matisse, Dufy, Derain and Picasso for example, had felt the necessity of the transfer from objective to subjective reality but none of them had as yet achieved his rigorous composition, the supremacy of what was represented over the innumerable temptations of what was seen, pretext though it might be. It was Braque alone who felt and solved so quickly and so soon this purely painterly problem, the rejection of everything anecdotal. He paints essentials and not accidentals. His poetic creation is not an addition, more or less incorporated in the technique of the work. They are not separable from each other because the technique contains the poetic creation and arrives at it by its own means. A picture, for Braque, is a closed world of painting which is sufficient unto itself. It is its own end.

Picasso, after the Blue and Rose Periods, from 1902 to 1905 and 1906, made the discovery, in company with Derain, of Negro and Polynesian masks. He immediately took this magical "expressionism" to himself, first as a lyrical plus-value and then, after the expressive phase, as a source of æsthetic forms. His painting in no way resembled that of Braque. His Negro Period lasted throughout the year 1908 and resulted in new formal possibilities but in a different direction to that taken by Braque.

A question of space certainly occupied Picasso but as a means of expression not as the absolute problem it was for Braque. It was not until 1909 at Horta del Ebro in Spain that, under the influence of the works of Cézanne's Gardanne period, he began to paint the geometrical landscapes which have something in common with Braque's work of 1907, 1908 and 1909, though not in coloring. Where the latter used greens, ochres and grays, Picasso preferred yellows and browns.

One point must be insisted on; pre-Cubism was quite a different thing from the Cubism of the years 1910 to 1914. Pre-Cubism was the slow discovery, starting from Cézanne, of elements amenable to geometric treatment. Cubism (wrongly socalled as it did not use cubes) consisted of objects used figuratively as ideas, represented simultaneously in their different geometrical possibilities with the appearances disassociated and perspective reduced to the two-dimensional level of the canvas. It is the imagined thing, added to the reality already plastically interpreted.

Picasso's Negro Period ended in Cubism but with a rapid change-over, as is his habit and not the progressive evolution of Braque. That his work influenced that of Braque in 1910 is not to be denied but it is equally true that the latter's achievements of 1907, 1908 and 1909 channeled Picasso's efforts into Cubism. Æsthetically speaking there is a greater distance between Picasso's *Mandolin Player* or his *Demoiselles d'Avignon* and his first Cubist painting than there is between Braque's *Still Life with Clarinet and Mandolin* (Pl. 19), the *L'Estaque Viaduct* (Pl. 13), *Port in Normandy* (Pl. 16), *Guitar and Fruit Dish* (Pl. 21), *Fishing Boats* (Pl. 15) or *La Roche-Guyon* (Pl. 18) of 1908 and his first truly Cubist pictures.

The problem which Braque set himself straightaway was that of *absolute* form and structure. The first work in which we see it dealt with is the 1908 landscape *Houses at L'Estaque* (Pl. 12).

The "pictorial fact" had attained its first profound realization. The subject was abolished in favor of the object; sensation (Impressionist, Fauve or otherwise) was replaced by construction. There was a new æsthetic system evolved which could only express itself in special figurative themes and was based entirely on rhythms, which had their source in Cézanne, were capable of variations and amenable to geometrical treatment. The objects had to be adequate in value to fit in with the principles of the æsthetic system, which was entirely plastic. Thus Juan Gris was able to say: "Out of a cylinder I make a bottle," in contradiction to Cézanne who thought of a bottle as a cylinder and made it so. We may note that to make a bottle out of a cylinder was practically Braque's idea of poetic creation, as when he said: "The splash of white turns into a tablecloth."

The period of 1907 to 1909 was for Braque the search for "filled space", without spatial divisions or depth of perspective and constructible within narrow dimensions, which should sum up by vertical juxtaposition the reality of the object-motifs.

Since the picture had to form a plastic total, a plastic correspondence had to be found between form and color. Cézanne had found it in adaptive modulation but this paid too much attention to objective facts and made the painting too dependent on reality, which was of no use to Braque. Forms and colors, for him, were two plastic themes to be united only by means of subordination, so that the rhythmic and volumetric unity of the picture could be built up. They were neither independent nor supplementary but complementary, two imagined conditions of the object, constructed in unity so that the plastic qualities of the picture should not be broken up, though this involved the reduction of the palette to a few colors only. At the end of 1907 and throughout the greater part of 1908, his palette consisted entirely of ochres and greens. At the end of 1908 and in 1909, Braque returned to individual tones for a particular object, not for any increase in objective reality but because he thought that, properly used, they could give an additional plastic element. He soon abandoned them, and the spatial problem appeared again, more imperatively than ever, perhaps because these "local" tones had turned out other than he thought and were susceptible of an evolution to be discovered later. Perhaps also they made him reconsider the nature of the object in terms of painting, and the problem of representing plastic form in all its diversity.

What both he and Picasso were looking for, was the pictorial polyvalency of the object, its integration in a space which should not be of three dimensions. It was, in fact, the problem of true Cubism, space which should represent both the object, the content and also the containing space.

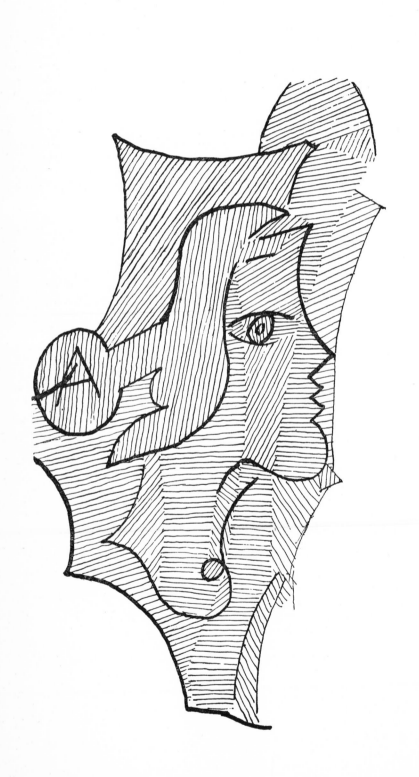

CUBISM FROM 1910 TO 1914

BRAQUE was Cubist before Picasso. His *Mandolin* of 1908 (Pl. 19) proves it. He already associated straight lines and curves, (the neck and sound-box of the mandolin); he knew, as Gleizes says, that "the curve is to the straight line as the warm tone is to the cold tone" and he knew also that the simple relationships of ochres and greens which are almost negative in space, or at least reduced to the essential structure, must indicate volumes contained in an imaginary container.

It was Picasso, the Neo-Romantic and above all the "Expressionist," who was influenced by Braque. As early as 1909 Picasso's *Pains*, his *Harlequin* and his *Woman in Green*, for example, were in Braque's manner. He seems to have acquired a discipline leading to a strict æsthetic system; but it was a discipline against which he would always be in revolt, while for Braque it was a necessity. Where one was an enthusiast and an anarchist, the other was reflective. What one discovered by his enthusiasm, the other concentrated into an æsthetic system, but the former profited by the discipline brought by the latter. Their work was complementary. To Picasso's fire, his anxiety, his temptations and his perpetual search, Braque contributed calm, continual meditation and confidence.

What Braque contributed to Cubism was so much that one may well ask if it could have existed without him. There would certainly have been Cubist works by Picasso but there would not have been the æsthetic system, the technique or the Cubist school which evolved continuously and progressively from 1910 to 1914. Cubism, after Fauvism, and after Gauguin's work in "limited space," and that of Seurat in "decomposed space," was a new and different reaction against Impressionism. For the dissociation of color in light and the disappearance of individual "local" tones in overall lighting, Cubism substituted the analytical dissociation of the object in a neutral light. It set out to find an equivalence between light and form; form was broken up into small planes, either lighted or luminous, with multiple facets. The volumetric structure was separated from its three spatial dimensions and reconstructed ideologically on the two dimensions of the canvas. The coloring of objects remained a problem because it implied a different and fixed form for the object, limited by color values, which was incompatible (at least at this period) with the special kind of polymorphous figuration which had been discovered.

In Braque's works from 1908 to 1909, which were more and more Cubist, the color problem was lost sight of beside the all-important problem of form. It was he who first found the solution to this in his *Woman with a Mandolin* (Pl. 21). He situates the different facets on the two-dimensional level of the canvas, so that the object is seen in all its possibilities, real or imaginable. Thickness is not indicated by *trompe-l'œil* but suggested only. The organized perspective of the Renaissance painters is abolished, not only as being useless but as being incompatible with the planned rhythm of the work. Forms are no longer to be seen or portrayed in the same perspective; on the contrary each element (true or imaginary) of the object must be observed at a particular angle and constructed so that it fits into the organized rhythm of the picture.

Space becomes a juxtaposition of images on different levels. Light is spread out over the different elements but the coloring is homogeneous, admitting only varying tones of earths, ochres, grays and olive greens. The drawing is sharpened up by reason of the intermingling of these facets on different levels. In fact it becomes anonymous, as each painter subscribes to the system without trying to affirm his personality.

In the choice of colors, Braque was the most subtle of them all, as he had been during his Fauve period. He used a mother-of-pearl full of light golds and ivory yellows which allowed him an extraordinary suppleness in composition for the establishment of his "filled space."

The object was thus analyzed in all its possibilities or fragments of its reality, which became elements of its construction. Just as Impressionism was the study of colored lighting, so Cubism was the study of the object in its total figurative capacity. Where the former sought to create a luminous whole, the latter did create a whole, no longer luminous but a representation of all the forms, true, possible or imaginary, of an object, in which light was not an essential but a complementary element in the reproduction and disposition of the structural facets. It was incorporated in the object but neither defined it nor constructed it.

The object thus becoming unique and preponderant replaced the subject which still existed in Impressionism, since atmosphere constituted its principal value. Dawn, daybreak, morning, midday, evening, summer, spring, autumn, winter, sun, mist and rain are anecdotal, sentimental themes since they have an effective resonance and give a descriptive and literary tone to the visual matter. Add to this the fact that every painter, according to his temperament, has a preference for a certain moment of the day or the year and that, often unconsciously, he exaggerates what he sees to the extent that he likes it or is moved by it, and one can see at once how literature and anecdote become tacked on to painting.

Cubism wished to be entirely objective and even if it was subjective in its ideology, the latter was neither sentimental nor anecdotal. The theme represented was not the subject of a work because it had as title: *Violin, Pitcher, Fruit Plate, Mandolin,* etc. The latter only indicated the possible identity of what was represented figuratively in the picture. These themes were more or less common to all the Cubist painters.

Cubism was first of all a discipline as a result of which personalities such as Braque, Picasso and Juan Gris stood out without resembling each other but sharing a common æsthetic system.

The final result of Cubism was not spectacular, it lay in the negation of a dead past and the birth of a new vision of the world which was strictly a painter's vision. The Cubist painters had been tempted by Fauvism, but all the same they had been absorbed by the objective reality of the world.

Cubism at its birth brought something new by going back to the origins of painting. Following Impressionism and Fauvism, it refused the contribution of the Renaissance painters, the spatial composition called perspective.

The painters of the Middle Ages knew nothing of perspective; they superimposed one fragment of a picture on another to make a global vision in which space was no more than an adventitious descriptive element. Neither Bosch nor Patinir nor Breughel emphasized perspective. For them a picture was necessarily a "concerted" vision, that is to say organized around a directive theme. Cubism did exactly the same. Setting out from a volumetric and rhythmic theme, it produced a plastic and decorative one, in fact in the long run a voluntary composition. It carried Cezanne's constructive aims to their logical conclusion.

Space in Cubism is Braque's "tactile space". The object, multiply represented, comes out from the painting toward the spectator instead of being separated from him in progressive depth. In its growing pursuit of tactile space, Cubism rejected landscape, which was bound up with visual space. Only an object, whatever its nature, could find a place in this new aesthetic system.

The few human figures painted by Braque during this period are pure human *objects*. Their component parts are treated like those of a guitar or a mandolin; they are never imitated but only used. In this domain of human figuration Braque has remained more severe than Picasso. For him a picture continues to be uniquely a *pictorial fact*.

But was this aesthetic system not to find itself at a dead end and the object-facet fall into repetition? Was there not a new, a kind of "pre-poetical" element necessary in its representation? Braque found this in the material of the painting. His memories of childhood and youth with his father and of his profession as a decorator gave birth to a most opportune intuition.

As his pictures lacked something evocative, he introduced lettering into their composition. His first Cubist picture with lettering is *Le Portugais* (Former Coll. Raoul Laroche; Pl. 26) where one finds the word BAL at the bottom in stencilled letters. This alphabetical figuration, which may seem an eccentricity, though it did not increase the meaning of the picture, which has none, did on the other hand give it an emotive plus value, which, though vague, was sufficient, with its resonances and allusions, to create a need for interpretation. And it was not only that; the three black letters of the word BAL have a painterly value and are not only a component tone in the work (as a spot of paint might be) but introduce what we may call a "pre-

lyrical" atmosphere, an "aura" which, without going beyond the work itself and connecting it with the banal literary associations of the word BAL, give it an expressive plus value.

These letters and all the others which follow added a kind of mystery to the purely plastic resonances. The word-sign which had no precise meaning in a picture, to which it seemed unrelated, became an as yet unsuspected possibility of interpretation.

This contribution of Braque's was of great importance. Picasso used letters of the alphabet but for other ends than Braque. He gave them the value of things, of a baroque addition, an "expressionist" supplement, while Braque only required them to be a starting point in the direction of a poetic super-reality.

Braque has used letters of the alphabet all his life, attaching to them different meanings and resonances. Here are a few examples: BAL and the number 1040 in *Le Portugais* (1911); — GIL B in the *Porte-allumettes* (1910. Roger Dutilleul Coll.); — *La Table du Musicien* (1913. Pl. 29); — the *Papier collé with the letters* JOH (1914. Marius de Zayas Coll., Stamford, Conn.); — the *Violin* (1914. Museum of Modern Art, New York); — *La Bouteille de Rhum* (1920. Coll. Mr. and Mrs. Joseph Pulitzer, St. Louis); — *Guitar with the letters* POLKA (1920. Pl. 43), and among many others the *Table ronde avec* ETUDE (1929. Pl. 55), and the *Nature Morte dite* LE JOUR (Pl. 60).

In the *Aria de Bach*, a *papier collé* of 1914 (Pl. 52), as in the 1937 *Duo* (National Museum of Modern Art, Paris. Pl. 94) the names of Bach and Debussy are used to indicate his musical tastes.

But lettering turning out to be insufficient, it was necessary to add other figurative elements, to avoid continually starting afresh, and it was Braque who introduced *papiers collés*. Insomuch as for him a picture was a *"pictorial fact"* resulting in a "poetic creation," there could be no "level of meaning" without a "level of appearance," so that it was on the latter that all investigation must be centered. From the differences in the "level of appearance" come the differences in the "level of meaning," and this was the role of the *papier collé*.

Up till then the so-called analytical Cubism had been in pursuit only of a new kind of space, obtained by the breaking up of an object into figurative elements susceptible of giving a total image which would be non-real since it was not subjected to trompe-l'œil. Color, as the tone of an object, ceased to exist; only such few tones were allowed which permitted variations of light but not colored shapes.

It was impossible to go any further and everything seemed to have been discovered, but the *papiers collés* brought a renewal of the expressive technique of pure Cubism without taking from the rigor of its composition. At the same time they enlarged the aesthetic system. For Braque the sand foundation which he discovered at the same time added to the technique by modifying the quantity and the quality of the paint and creating a further level of appearance.

The introduction of *papier collé* (and for Picasso, pieces of other materials as well) reintegrated the reality of an object in a picture by a piece of the object itself. Rhythmic and plastic organization had to be recomposed and given a new structure. The material nature of the "foreign body" called for a corresponding flexibility in its surroundings, so that it should be integrated in the rhythmic total which must on no account be lost sight of. It must become "other" while submitting to obligations either of dispersion or concentration. If the material reality of the object regained importance for the spectator, it must, however, neither deny nor refute what had been previously acquired but add to it.

The consequences of this re-objectivization of color led the original analytical Cubism to the stage of what Juan Gris called synthetic Cubism. At least as far as Picasso was concerned, and for Braque too, it was not an end but a transition and an enrichment.

For him, the juxtaposition of *papier collé* with its surroundings was made cautiously. In the very complicated *Still Life with Playing Cards* (1913. Pl. 34), the cards, the letters and the bunch of grapes are drawn and done in gouache; there is color apart from that of the *papier collé*. In the *Courrier*, also 1913, the COURRIER is a newspaper and as well as the wallpaper around it, there are barely indicated a circle and a diamond. Letters and colors are associated. In the *Clarinette* (1913. Former Coll. Ozenfant), we find all on one canvas, a newspaper "L'ECHO D'A..." and a complicated wallpaper drawn in charcoal and colored in chalk and oils. Color is more fully used and in the *Statue d'Epouvante* (the title of a film), a picture belonging to Picasso, only the program and the wallpapers are *papier collé*, all the rest, including a sketched-in guitar in the middle, are drawn. The same applies to *Tivoli Cinema*, another stuck-on bill (Pl. 32). From 1913 on Braque returned to painting only. The *Music Score* (Pl. 29) is entirely painted, and so are the *Guitarist with the letters* LE REVEIL *and* SONATE, the *Composition with the letters* JOH (1914) and *The Violin* of the same year. The predominance of color, or at least of paint, is reasserted.

A further contribution of Braque's, tried out since 1912, was the preparation of a canvas with sand mixed into the paints. The quantity and density of the material was thereby increased and it engendered a certain quality of color and light. The result was a granulation (which reminds one of certain pictures of Cézanne — *La Maison du Pendu* — and of Chardin). The color, when put on, acquires multiple possibilities of capturing atmospheric light and reflections, which gives it an intensity it would not otherwise have.

Picasso too sought chromatic weight by the use of impasto, as for example *A Violin* (1913. Rupf Coll., Berne) in which he thickens the curves of a guitar's sound box in order the better to frame the blue tuning parts with the *f* of a violin.

It was now the year 1914 and the eve of the war. Cubism seemed to have attained its essential objectives and we may perhaps sum up its accomplishment, particularly in the work of Braque.

The Fauve period had been no more for him than the discovery of the fundamental elements of painting: a formal construction in which the predominance of color gave a picture the violence of shock. Braque wanted and sought for something different. He is certainly intuitive but even more a constructor of form. He tends always toward a deep study of what comes up through instinct in order to arrive at an articulate organization. In the case of a picture, that is to say a representation in two dimensions of a space which has three, it is space which must be acted on and reduced to the dimensions of the picture.

This space does not penetrate into the third dimension, it is inscribed on the level of the canvas which it fills up and the investigation of the question, which was earlier than Cubism and began in 1908 and 1909, resulted in a Cubism which was the first realization of an ideological absolute insomuch as it proclaimed itself to be no more than a "laying-out" and "making-up" of the plastic possibilities of the problem.

Classical perspective goes from the level of the canvas toward the background and is accomplished by trompe-l'œil, chiaroscuro, foreshortening and the subterfuge of lines all converging on a vanishing point at the horizon-line, etc... Cubist perspective goes from the surface level of the canvas toward the spectator; the figurative elements are painted by facets with different orientations and, later, by planes coupled one behind the other. The ensemble of the construction goes from the canvas outward, toward the person looking at it. For the ideology to be best realized in the construction, at least from 1913 on, the background from which the figurations detach themselves is a plane, a sort of wall without any space possible behind it. The Cubist suggestion of space is thus attained.

Analytical Cubism began by dissociating form and color. Braque soon felt and understood that this dissociation, if not a total error, announced a deficiency, whence his anxiety and his search for a "relationship" to unite form and color in a plastic simultaneity and for which, abandoning monochrome, he reintroduced color by means of *papiers collés*, and then painted them in trompe-l'œil instead of actually including them.

He was admirably served by a technique of which he knew all the resources through his apprenticeship as a painter-decorator. He knew how to paint imitation wood and imitation marble and how to put on thick coats and thin coats; the composition of color shades was no secret to him and he inserted with the greatest of ease the lettering whose decorative as well as indicative value was as familiar to him as that of wallpaper framed by a layer of paint. From this knowledge there came, in his subsequent work, the decorated walls and color harmonies which are those of a decorator of apartments. With this craftsman's technique, in addition to the plastic values of the color combinations, there is an aesthetic value: each picture is bathed in a light which is not directed but "thickened" so that each color becomes a plastic "*fact*." It is developed object by object so that they are integrated into the total composition which is the picture. The "local" or individual tone is not commanded by the reality of the "thing represented" but becomes a particular condition associated rhythmically with the others. It is purified both from representation and from imitation.

Braque has been reproached with the varying figuration of the objects he paints. The reproach is founded on Cubist ideology; there can be no question of *this* glass, *this* guitar, *this* mandolin, *this* fruit dish, etc. The object must be an abstract, a *schema* of the real, almost a Platonic *idea*, and not a fabricated reality, The idea of a glass replaces the reality of glasses.

If one looks carefully at the glasses reproduced in Braque's work, one finds that they are all reduced to the schematic image of a certain "glass in itself" which he chose because it expressed not only its essence but a particular form which, as *such*, incorporated itself plastically in the work. It is only an occasional variant and not a final abstraction, a plastic and not an ideological element. The same might be said about all the other objects he painted because Braque is a painter and not a theorist.

Since Braque and Picasso were the inventors of Cubism and quite a few of their works have been confused, those of one being attributed to the other, and this all the more easily as they only signed their work on the back, it may be useful to compare some of their pictures between 1908 and 1914.

PICASSO	BRAQUE
1908	1908
FAMILY OF HARLEQUINS	HOUSES AT L'ESTAQUE
(1.90 × 0.81 meters). Coll. Baron von der Heydt, Ascona (Switzerland).	(0.73 × 0.60 meters) (Pl. 12). Coll. Rupf, Berne.
Pre-Cubist picture deriving from the Negro Period.	A pre-Cubist picture deriving from Cézanne's constructive principles.
Tonality: gray, brown, mauve, greyish, browns and greens.	Tonality: gray-violet (tree tones), greens and ochres.

1909

SEATED WOMAN

(0.99 × 0.81 meters). Coll. Penrose, London.

Painted in greens near to browns, grays with dominant blues or greens, and browns tending toward yellow.

1911-1912

THE CLARINET-PLAYER

(1.60 × 0.67 meters). Coll. Douglas Cooper, London.

A light brown monochrome tending to yellow with varying small touches.

1913

THE VIOLIN

(0.65 × 0.40 meters). Coll. Rupf, Berne.

The *f*'s of the violin are in planes of blue. Underneath on the side, imitation wood.

Here and there, indications of the double curve of a guitar's sound box painted thick.

1909-1910

VIOLIN AND JUG

(1.16 × 0.73 meters) (Pl. 23). Coll. Laroche; Basel, Kunstmuseum.

Monochrome of gray greens with yellows. A nail with its shadow painted at the top of the canvas makes for a *true* reality.

1911

LE PORTUGAIS

(0.81 × 0.46 meters). Coll. Laroche; Kunstmuseum, Basel.

Various warm browns with little square touches. The first appearance of painted letters and numbers, BAL and 1040.

1914

ARIA DE BACH

(0.46 × 0.35 meters) Coll. Mme Cuttoli, Paris.

The background is gray. Very fine drawing with a Conté pencil. Two black engraved tuning-parts and one wood-brown.

If one compares the respective contributions of Picasso and Braque, one finds that, with a similar technique used for an identical aesthetic ideology, what differentiates the Spanish from the French master is the lyrical quality. That of Picasso is composed of the aggressive positions he took up and his spectacularly affective values, whereas Braque's is reflective; he took up no violent positions, but they succeeded each other in growth. His pictures are an approach to poetic creation.

Picasso's *Family of Harlequins*, deriving from the Negro Period, has an expressionist lyrical quality. Braque's *Houses at L'Estaque* is the first result of the study of Cézanne's constructive principles.

In volume and color Picasso's *Seated Woman* is dynamic, which is a form of expressionism. Braque's *Violin and Jug* (Pl. 23) is a purely static plastic construction.

Picasso's *Clarinet-Player* is aggressive, not by its lyricism but by its extreme schematization and its allusions. Braque's *Le Portugais* (Pl. 36) is of great figurative complexity, both by its planes and by the introduction of lettering and numbers, new elements of composition which were to result in a poetic super-reality, etc...

Thus, from Cubism on, the personalities of Picasso and Braque became separate and opposite. Picasso is a neo-Romantic, Baroque Spaniard; Braque is a Frenchman for whom classicism is a necessity.

Cubism was thus a re-objectivization of the object. It was content at first with an equivalence of light by its identification with reflections and planes, identification and superimposition whose aim was to construct the object according to the two dimensions of the canvas only.

It is remarkable also that Cubism, however much it innovated in the purely ideological field, was a dead end. This is well known. It gave birth on the one hand to Picasso's *abstract* painting and on the other to his surrealism. A return to the object, not realist but simply "indicated," was seen to be a necessity. First Braque, then Picasso, and Juan Gris very strongly, understood this. The lettering as well as the *papiers collés* were part of a search for it.

As "foreign bodies" the *papiers collés* disappeared, soon to be replaced by their appearance in paint. This reintroduced, as we have seen, the color value of the objects and that reintroduction led to others. This was perhaps the reason why after 1912-1913 Braque and Picasso partially adopted Seurat's technique of small colored spots, his "confetti," which did not destroy the "space level" because they were introduced in depth. They thickened even more the density of the plane (cf. Pl. 36 and 38).

Braque, moreover, understood their value as he had used them during his Fauve period.

It is wrong to think that Cubism died in 1914. On the contrary it took on a prodigious new life in the following years.

30

A NEW CUBISM

AUGUST 1914. Picasso as a Spaniard was not mobilizable but Sergeant Georges Braque left for the front. There he had a magnificent record, well in keeping with his character: to be totally and valuably what one must be. He was twice mentioned in dispatches and was badly wounded in the head, necessitating a trepanning. In 1917 he was invalided out.

Was he to paint again? How indeed should he not do so? Painting was his entire life. The problem was not whether to paint, but what and how to paint.

What had painting become in the last three years, and particularly that painting which was so profoundly his own, Cubism?

Picasso had painted pictures resulting from Cubism, with lettering and pointillism à la Seurat. In 1915 he had begun the Harlequins which were to last until 1920, related by their costume of colored diamonds to the facets of Cubism. He also painted the *Guéridons* (pedestal tables), and in 1916 *L'Homme à la Pipe* and variations on these themes. But what was most characteristic in his work was an "ornamented" Cubism, begun in 1914 and whose masterpiece was to be the *Femme sur Fond Vert* of 1919. Braque had to begin again from where he had left off, taking into account what had been done by others.

If one compares the works of Picasso with those of Braque in these next three years, one cannot but notice both the similarities and the differences. The similarities were inevitable because Braque was beginning, the differences were inherent because he was continuing his own work, and showed what he had been rather than what he wanted to be.

He began anew in order to get his bearings, to find himself again, even though his work resembled that of others. He continued by "experiments with a view to improvement," feeling his way toward resonances in his work, of which he had no knowledge but only a presentiment. The fundamental problem of painting had not changed for him: the pictorial fact in a pictorial space. Cubism, insofar as it sought for this kind of space, was never to be forgotten. It would be enriched, transformed and submit to such mutations as were necessary. The continuity of Braque's work is proof of this. What had been done directed what was being done and what remained to be accomplished.

From 1917 on, a new Cubism was on the rise, that of *painted wallpapers* and *wall backgrounds* which were at the same time a search for color and rythm and for a picture space suggested by small juxtaposed dabs of paint, serving to separate objects from the beholder.

The Goblet or *The Guitar* (Pl. 36), of 1917-1918, both contained in octagons, are on panels, and the drawing has as much importance as the painting. The *Woman with a Mandolin* (1917. Pl. 34) has elements of pointillist workmanship. The *Still Life with Grapes and the letters* RNAL of 1918 is inserted in an oval frame; pointillism is used but in a different way from Picasso, as it looks like a wallpaper. The *Still Life with a Guitar* of the Kröller-Müller museum (Pl. 37) is contained in a diamond, *La Bouteille de Rhum* in an oval.

The new Cubism announced itself in 1918, notably in the *Still Life with the letters* RNAL (0.49 × 0.63 meters), which is an oval in breadth, the *Bouteille de Rhum* (0.99 × 0.70 meters) a vertical oval, a painted canvas on which one finds the ace of clubs and wallpapers, and a first *Table with Still Life* (Basel museum; 1.30 × 0.75; Pl. 59), a forerunner of the *guéridons* and tables of later years. In all these works the tactile space appears more and more in the construction.

A surprising picture, the large figure of the *Musicienne* (2.40 × 1.10 meters; Pl. 35) comes into this experimental period by reason of its ornamental wallpaper. In its composition, which is almost entirely vertical with wide rectangles crossed only by the instrument and the two hands, its very real imitation wood and no less real imitation linoleum and floor-mosaic, and above all the intervention of the background walls in the space construction, it is the principal work of 1918.

That of 1919 was to be *Café-Bar* (which belongs like the former to the Basel museum, also enriched by the gift of the Raoul Laroche collection). It is one of the masterpieces of this period, which show Braque's emancipation.

In this same year of 1919, Picasso painted the *Fillette au Cerceau, Ecolière*, and the *Chevalet sur un Guéridon*. The flat tones are of a sharp violence in contrast or opposition, a violence which may be due to the influence of the decors and costumes of the Ballet Russe for whom he had been working. The aesthetic and technique are still Cubist with superposed planes. But they are different from those of Braque, whose coloring is no less lively but more balanced by neighboring resonances. Moreover Braque's painting material is powerful, thick and, it too, made rhythmic by neighboring values.

While Picasso's Catalan fieriness kept his work intuitively expressionist and aggressive in appearance, that of Braque grew by profound and constructive reflection. The differences in the Spanish and French were national genius became more and more clear. Picasso's pictures are always lyrical explosions and by temperament he never ceases to despise reality; those of Braque are concentrated meditations with a view to the poetic creation to be attained.

Some of these works were shown in 1919 (March 5-31) at Léonce Rosenberg's Galerie de l'Effort Moderne in Paris.

To terminate, I should like to examine the *Café-Bar* in order to situate correctly the evolution of Braque's work.

In this work (Pl. 40) we still find the Cubist aesthetic system but with a distinct difference. Space is constituted by overlapping planes (Cubism) but the lines which draw the eye are those used particularly by Braque to obtain plenitude and density. The table and the objects which it supports are framed in a tall rectangle with tones and drawing propagated from the bottom upwards. The tonality of the frame is gray and black with very somber brown tints. The objects are bare indications: a guitar, a fruit-dish with fruit, a newspaper, a pipe and a music score.

As with Picasso, the totality of the picture is the plastic sum of the objects; that is to say the pretexts and motifs and the sum of their figuration, which one may describe as follows: "object seen from in front plus object seen from the side plus object seen sectionally, and from both above and below etc...", to which may be added: "object in the rhythm of the plane plus object in the rhythm of the curve etc...". The difference from Picasso resides in the fact that there is no plastic concentration on figuration and the relationships which exist by dint of proximity are not confined to the objects. Around them is a space which is also objectivized and made rhythmic, the large gray-black quadrilateral is *filled in* and there are the color-values of the fruit-dish with its fruit, the table and the newspaper; while the grays and blacks| of the background are dependent on the music score and the pipe. All that Braque was to paint subsequently, and paints to this day, is present in this picture, either actually or potentially.

The picture is, in all respects, a form constructed by multiple relationships between the objects and the background. What one might call the differential forms of each object imply those of others. Thus the plane of green with horizontal patches of orange (on the level of the foot of the table and on the rectangular check carpet) frames, here and there, the guitar and the fruit-dish. The checks of the carpet change into points and half-diamonds at the top of the canvas.

That the picture is still Cubist cannot be denied. But there is something else, which we shall find later in the paintings with figures: the *Duo*, the *Femme peintre*, *L'Atelier*, etc...

Thus in 1918, back from the war and healed of his wounds, Braque began to paint again and found the future components of his works in what he still retained of Cubist formulas. I must insist once more on *Café-Bar* in that it does afford a prefiguration of the work to come; the background already participates in the general rhythm and, as such, marks the beginning of *total space*.

Let us return to *visual space* which, for Braque, is the separation of objects, one from another, by a gap. The gap can only be known by us through our eyes and through all that is connoted psycho-physiologically by vision. The objects are not immediately accessible to the hand; one must go toward them and is a from one to another.

It is otherwise with tactile space, which does not separate us from objects and objects from each other in the same way as visual space. The object-motifs, or pretexts, of a still life are close to us, neighboring one another, accessible and within reach of our hands. What separates them is not a vision of space but an act of approach. They form a reduced, circumscribed space in which they are plastically juxtaposed.

In *Café-Bar* the *visual space* barely exists. The background is close to the objects, behind them but right up against them. Moreover it is not of a different rhythmic nature, and consequently not a spatial element, the container of what is contained, i.e. the objects. It is their consequence, their continuance, and a plastic enlargement around them. In this way the *tactile or total space*, in other words *pictorial space*, participant; and it is this which definitely separates Braque from Picasso.

In 1922 Braque was forty. The appearance of the *Cheminée* (Chimney-piece and fire-place) series, in which tactile space and a form of total space are attained, marks a decisive stage in his work.

Let me describe the *Cheminée* of 1922 (Pl. 50).

The Chimney-piece goes up a little higher than half the canvas. It is painted in "imitation marble" carefully and realistically. It supports a guitar, a bowl of grapes and behind them a bottle of which only the neck is visible above the beginning of the body of the instrument. Then comes another bowl of fruit (two pears). And up against it are wallpapers and a score "Duo".

The still life is painted according to the Cubist manner.

How, we may ask, in this amazing canvas, are pictorial space and tactile space constructed? For the supreme aim of the work is the co-existence of these two spaces:

I. *Pictorial space*. It is necessarily constructed according to the two-dimensional space level. They must project the objects in front of the canvas. It is here that double figuration comes in, realist for the chimney-piece and cubist for the still life on top of it.

a) The level of the canvas, a two-dimensional surface, is the upper background, the wallpaper. b) The Cubist still life is situated in front of it on three planes: the score, the fruit dish with pears; the plane of the bottle; and that of the guitar and the grape bowl. c) Now this Cubist still life rests on the realistic figuration of the chimney-piece. The realistic figuration also implies the *spatial image* of the chimney-piece and thus increases the effect of depth due to the three superposed planes of the Cubist still life.

There is something else as well: the line of vision. It is situated very high, on the level of the top of the bottle and the edge of the pear dish. It is clearly indicated and gives a view from above. The mantle of the chimney-piece can only be a line; for one's eyes, which reconstruct the natural perspective, it appears to climb from the foreground to the background, which suggests a space in depth for the Cubist still life. In addition the chimney-piece is painted slightly askew, going up from the right to the left which creates another indication of depth. The dark patch or the fire-back and the white embrasure which surrounds it accentuate the indication.

These successful artifices allow Braque to construct a total pictorial space, projecting itself forward in three movements: 1) the wall which pushes the still life toward the spectator, 2) the still life which develops on three planes, 3) the chimney-piece which completes the imaginable space.

This space is a *full* space, without voids, a space with joined figurations. It is also a visual space by reason of the realistic painting of the chimney-piece from which we are separated by a void. Thus the

void which is absent in the juxtaposition of the painted objects, exists, outside the picture and in front of it, between it and us.

II. *Tactile space :* It depends entirely on the pictorial space, that masterly indication of space, and this, firstly because there is a void between the picture and ourselves, in front of it, secondly because the three-plane construction of the still life implies a suggestion of depth; but the objects are separated from each other and can thus, in imagination, be touched in definitely situated places.   Touchable, that is to say, by possible gestures, short or prolonged, not only imaginable or imagined, but felt.

Although it is later, 1927, I will analyze another *Cheminée* so as to compare them (Pl. 49).

It is presented differently.   The chimney-piece properly speaking is seen from in front.   It has no imitation marble.   It is less realistic than the preceding picture.   The still life which it supports is such as Braque painted them from 1923-1924 on.

From right to left: the guitar, and a fruit dish with a bunch of grapes.   Behind: a music score.   Behind that, a glass and wallpaper, and finally a large width of wall.   In the foreground on the left, there is a narrow rectangle which ascends from the bottom of the canvas to the base of the fruit dish.

34

I. *Pictorial space.* The level of the canvas is no longer the background wall; it is imposed by the tall narrow rectangle. The whole figuration is situated behind it and at a certain distance. There is a *suggestion of true spaces*: 1) A filled-up space, that of the chimney-piece and of the still life; 2) An empty space which separates the chimney-piece from the foreground imposed by the rectangle.

As in the preceding picture, the still life is projected forward by the plane of the wall. The line of vision is lower than in the other picture, which should imply a greater foreshortening, but there is nothing of the sort. On the contrary the picture is deeper because Braque has much reduced the height of the mantelpiece by a distortion, necessary in constructing the space of the still life.

In this still life, the figuration of objects by volumes no longer follows the Cubist absolute. The objects have thickness or depth, the guitar as well as the fruit dish and the music score which is open in a very wide V. The painter seems to have wished to present a well-grouped still life and to give it its full value he had to situate it volumetrically in a space.

A too realistic and too detailed painting of the chimney-piece would have harmed the still life because it would be a partial element of a whole. The chimney-piece is reduced to the rôle of a table or a table support. It has another rôle which we shall see.

The picture space is thus as follows: 1) A background wall, very varied, in four vertical zones. It has a *participating* rôle, while in the preceding *Cheminée*, its values were only that of radiation. 2) A still life strongly constructed by volumes in space. It is the central mass which makes the balance and draws attention. Its balance of immobility and strength depends entirely on the linear disposition of the wall, the chimney-piece and the rectangle, and also on the fact that it alone is highly colored, all the rest being only a framing decor. 3) A rather wide gap between the chimney-piece plus still life group, and the level of the canvas imposed by the rectangle.

The result of this spatial composition is immediate. A considerable depth is established, a depth from which the still life benefits by a recession to the back of the foreground. There is, at the same time, *tactile space* and *visual space*.

II. *Tactile space.* It is double. 1) The objects of the still life are clearly separated from each other by suggestions of volume; and 2) they are separated from the spectator by the void between the level of the canvas (that of the rectangle) and the vertical plane of the fire-place. The still life is set forth in apprehensible dimensions.

III. *Visual space.* It is also double. 1) It goes from the foreground to the chimney-piece and 2) from the chimney-piece to the background wall.

This *Cheminée* provokes further reflections on the component parts of its "webwork."

A) *Vertical components.* By these I mean the lines of planes which ascend perpendicularly to the base of the picture. They may have a decisive importance. Certain vertical pictures such as *Le Poêle*, 1943 (Pl. 111) with its characteristic dimensions (1.46 × 0.89), the *Kitchen*, 1942, in the Paulhan Collection, or *La Toilette aux Carreaux Verts* (1.65 × 0.80; Pl. 114) for example—and we shall come across others— are uniquely constructed by these vertical components. In the *Cheminée* they are clearly to be seen. 1) The partitioning in four zones of the background wall with, in addition, the vertical fluting in the second zone from the right; 2) The construction lines of the mantelpiece; 3) The tall rectangle.

B) *Horizontal components.* I refer to the lines or parallel planes at the base of the picture. They too may have a decisive importance in the dimensions of the canvas, chosen for width.

In the picture which we were studying, the horizontal components, the mantelpiece and the top of the rectangle seemed to have no other purpose than to emphasize its marked verticality and to form the foundation on which the still life is developed.

Now, if one looks at the still life only, one notices that it is almost entirely constructed by *constituent curves*: the guitar and its incurving neck, the fruit dish, the apple, the grapes and the glass. Opposed to these curves and behind them are the straight lines of the music score and the wallpaper. All these curves are surrounded by lines or vertical and horizontal planes drawn by straight lines. They are the spectacular plus value which draws the attention to the still life. This process is often employed by Braque.

The right corner of the chimney-piece is also a curve, and as such breaks the dryness of the straight lines which construct it, balances by contrast the rigidity of the rectangle and is an addition to the still life, which it supports and balances.

I said above that the chimney-piece has another rôle besides that of table support. It is as follows: the still life is a typical creation of Braque in its division into two zones, one light (white), the other in color, the object in fact. Look at the guitar, the score and the fruit dish. The splay of the chimney-piece round the hood of the fire-place recalls this division. It is also a propagation and a variation, an additional touch of balance as it gives weight to the canvas toward the bottom and clearly situates the vertical plane of the chimney-piece by separating it from that created by the tall rectangle.

This magnificent picture is one of those which show most clearly the flowering of Braque's genius. It is himself. It attains the double aim which he seeks: the "pictorial fact", inserted in pictorial space, resulting in a poetic creation. It is remarkable, but to attain this (though other solutions appear later) he was obliged, from 1923 to 1924 on, both to re-create Cubism and return to a certain true reality, let us call it the natural reality of the object. It could not have been otherwise.

Cubist space was a dead end. Braque wanted an a pictorial space which would be in its totality a visual space, a separation in increasing depth, and a tactile space, a bringing together by juxtaposition. The return to the volume of the object, not "true" but strongly indicated, was the only solution, as it implied the tactile space, of which the visual space, in the still lifes, was no more than a trick of composition until it became the primary constituent of the "landscapes." He also wanted his work to constitute a poetic creation, that is to say that the figuration of the objects should attain a super-reality of meaning. Super-reality implies a reality to be transcended but, all the same, a reality.

Before continuing, let us take a look at Picasso's work in the years 1920-1923, in order to show what separated him more and more from Braque.

In 1920 Picasso began the period called "Antique" or "Roman," with gigantic figures of a powerful heavy realism, whose heads have a Greek profile with globulous, slightly protruding eyes, very tight lips and whose small hands have sausage-shaped fingers. The women's breasts are insolent, hard and taut. A typical example is the *Two Seated Nudes* (1920) in the Reber Collection. In this same year he also painted pre-historical anatomies, such as the *Baigneuses* whose thin conical necks rise to tiny, barely indicated heads with sparse, stiff hair. In 1921 *Two Seated Nudes* repeats the preceding theme but treating only the bone structure. In 1923 there is *The Beach* with equally distorted figures. Then comes a period of realism with a precious idyllic charm, with a simple graphism in an allusive setting of a ravishing purity which is "mannered," with or without relief; a sort of drawing enhanced by bright tones. *The Lovers, The Greek Woman, The Acrobat Resting* and the four large *Baigneuses* are half way between gigantism and mannerism, reminiscent of Renoir in many points, and even of the Venus of Milo.

In 1921 Picasso also painted, at Fontainebleau, the two hallucinating versions of the *Three Masked Musicians*, which take us back to Cubism. From 1919-1923, Picasso's Cubism was a return to the likeness of the object. He introduced graphisms by curves, colored planes and numerous "blacks."

We are a long way from Braque. Picasso continued to be his essential self, varying from moment to moment, with lyrical or athletic explosions. Braque perfected his work and attained the aim he sought. The difference in their work is a deep one. Picasso's Cubism as well as his Realism are more and more part of expressionist Surrealism. Braque's Cubism is transcended and amplified and tends more and more to a poetic super-reality.

Of this super-reality, which marks the flowering of his whole genius, the *Still Lifes* which Braque painted from 1923 on, and which developed after 1926 into versions where the supporting table is more and more frequently found, offer a masterly realization.

They are numerous and it is impossible to reproduce here as many as one would like and to list them would be sterile and tedious. We are taking a few as examples. (It may be noted that Christian Zervos reproduced 52 in the special number of "*Cahiers d'Art*" at the time of the 1933 Exhibition.)

First of all the *Still Life with Jug and Music Score*, 1924 (Pl. 52). The forward projection in accordance with Cubist ideology is affected by the plane of the wall, "the wallpaper." The line of vision is half way up the picture. A visual space is created between the level of the canvas and the plane of the wall. In the visual space the still life is painted by indicated volumes. The top of the bottle throws a shadow on the wall. There is thus visual space and tactile space. Pictorial space is also created by

36

the void suggested between the plane of the wall and the level of the canvas. It is both visual space (the void) and tactile space: the three planes on which the objects are situated.

The *Bottle and Pears* (1914; Pl. 51) has the same constituents. There is a difference to be stressed: the objects (pears, apples, glass and bottle) are no longer disposed in parallel planes but in an enveloping circle. One turns from the pears to the apples, from the apples to the glass, from the glass to the bottle, from the bottle to the apple, the napkin, with its curved forms being an addition in the gyration. The whole of the still life is thus a component curve in between the vertical implications of the background wall and the horizontal ones of the table, which is slightly askew and painted in imitation marbled wood.

For the *Still Life with Waltz* (1926; Pl. 53) Braque returned to Cubist figuration, but not entirely. The still life (music-book, fruit-dish and glass) is on the same plane; fruit-dish and glass have only indicated volume; in front and on the right of the "Waltz" is a pear in two zones, with its shadow on the table, above a fork. The space is in three planes : the wall, the still life and the level of the canvas. The tactile space is reduced to a minimum. The suggested volumes of the crumpled score, the fruit-dish with its upper half-curve and the glass with its curves indicated, present figurative contours but not a true contact. The predominant components, both vertical and horizontal, are rectilinear.

In all this richness of experimentation, *Two Apples and a Cup* is extraordinary in its simplicity. It is a "close-up" of two apples, a cup and a spoon. There is no visual space and no background, except touches of color. Space is tactile to a maximum degree. This still life is related to another of the same year, with *Pears and Knife*.

French art lovers had the privilege of seeing at the Still Life Exhibition at the Orangerie, in 1952, a very fine painting of 1927, *The Black Rose* (Pl. 57) (Coll. Mrs. Burton Tremaine, Jr.).

Although developed in width, the horizontal components of the work are not predominant. They are allied to multiple component curves. The background neither creates value nor participates; it limits the tactile depth. The pictorial space is fully realized, but by return to Cézanne's space. The depth is small and visual space is created by this depth. Tactile space is brought to a maximum point. Each of the objects is separated from us by a distance, and all are separated from each other.

The Canephorae

Without interrupting his pursuit of "space" in the still lifes, and indeed intensifying it in those with tables, Braque had begun in 1923 the series of Canephorae or basket-carriers, nude or semi-nude figures which carry a basket on the shoulder, if they are standing, or on the thigh if they are seated.

The *Canephorae* are vertical pictures, which implies a particular composition. Some have found a resemblance in them to Renoir's nudes and Gauguin's women, and a parallel with the nudes of Picasso's "Antique" period. I hardly believe in the influence of Renoir or Gauguin. Why should it have appeared in 1923? And there is no similarity and nothing in common with the work of Picasso. That Picasso's increasingly realist volumes should have incited Braque to paint the nudes, is very possible, if only to assert the fact that his conception, as a painter, of the female body was different, because for him it was not a pretext for erotic allusions, but only a plastic object with no significance beyond a superposition of round contours.

The Canephorae and the paintings which followed them were done between 1922 and 1926. Their ample forms, with anatomically precise muscles, at least in the torso, are on a large, carefully modeled scale. Their coloring is relatively dull: yellows and purples. White and gray are juxtaposed in the linen. No expression should be sought in their faces and no sexual emphasis in their bodies. It seems as if by their passiveness and neutrality, they make one with the fruit which fills their baskets. Renoir painted female nudes, flowers and fruit as three aspects of a desirable, sensual texture. Braque paints feminine bodies with their precise contours as he paints fruits in their geometric or geometrizable roundness. It is never the body of a certain woman or a female body as such: it is *the* female body, the motif of a plastic composition and a poetic creation.

The nude canephorae are either standing or seated. Noble and powerful as are the standing figures (often life-size), the most beautiful to me are those seated. The *Nude with Basket of Fruit* (Pl. 46) and the *Woman with Basket of Fruit* (Pl. 45) were painted respectively in 1924 and 1926. They are draped figures with unbound hair bearing the basket on the thigh. The *Nude with Basket of Fruit* is modeled by powerful shading. The *Woman with Basket of Fruit* is drawn in surface relief with white touches on a background of imitation marble.

This series, which has been called the "classical" figures, also produced a wonderful series of studies in crayon and pastel.

Under the influence of the fruit basket in the Canephorae Braque from 1923-1925 painted vases and baskets of flowers. After having painted different species, he came to prefer *Anemones*. (cf. notably Pl. 58) in which, for their variety of color, with an identical form, he found exactly what he was looking for: variations on a theme. In those of 1925, in one particularly, painted in oil and sand on canvas, the flowers, the leaves and the basket are concentrated in tones of russet and violet.

Soon to appear were marine themes: mussels and above all oysters and lemons. There are still today still lifes on these themes on the artist's easels.

The Tables

The year 1928 (and part of 1929) was that of the large compositions with pedestal tables for which Braque changed his palette. The browns, dark greens and the white were replaced by yellows, "tan" reds, blues, light greens and blacks. The wallpapers and the wood-tones also acquired a new importance.

As we can only reproduce a few of these, let us study one of the most characteristic.

The *Pedestal Table* (1926; Pl. 56) is a vertical picture (1.35 × 0.73 meters) in which the constituent curves predominate over the vertical components.

Still Life. It is very complicated with its overlappings and Cubist figurations, but it is Cubism with "variations" on the constituent curves. The usual three planes are in fact reduced to two: the apples and, under them, a rectangle on the right and the commencement of a newspaper on the left; then the body of the mandolin; and finally a second plane very mixed up: a gray fruit dish, a yellow fruit dish and the neck of the mandolin.

The whole still life is on a tray, of which the curved figurative element can be seen on the left. At the bottom, the end of a tablecloth hangs down.

Visual space. If one took the still life only into account, this would be short by reason of the vertical distortion of the top of the table, but the space which separates the level of the canvas from the plane in which the table is situated, increases it. It is deep underneath the table and short above it.

Tactile space. Very reduced. The two levels of the still life are too overlapping for us to be able to speak of true tactile space.

Pictorial space. It is markedly coherent in the still life and almost classical underneath it.

Rhythmic constituents. Although this is a vertical picture, the vertical components are not inwoven. The verticality of the work is determined only by the general assent of the figuration: the foot of the table, the planes of the pedestal and the still life and the two background planes which recall the preceding picture. The horizontal components are suggested. The constituent curves are multiple: the double foot of the table, and its fluted ball; the tablecloth; the large patch of gray; the whole still life and the angles of the top of the table. The *oblique* components, also multiple, are found in the still life.

Coloring. One can count seven tonalities, with "variations."

1) Numerous grays in the still life: the fruit dish, the plane and drawings of the apples on the right and the large curving plane below. 2) White: the hanging tablecloth, the patches next to the mandolin and between the gray fruit dish and the yellow one. 3) Yellows: a large part of the mandolin (yellow tending to pink), and the central fruit dish. 4) Blacks: the surroundings of the mandolin, the left background plane, part of the pedestal, and the linoleum with its black and white checks. 5) Browns: the ball-foot of the table, a right angle of the table, central fragments of the mandolin and the commencement of a newspaper. 6) Tan yellows: the background around the two planes and, in a darker shade, the right and left extremities of the pedestal and the floor. 7) Blue: the left background plane which reappears at the bottom, also on the pedestal and against the ball-foot of the table.

The constructive harmony of all these is very light and, as it were, joyful. The surface relations which diversify and situate them are developed with rare subtlety, as they give predominance to none and step each other up. One might, however, say that the yellow of the central fruit dish is the center of balance of all chromatic values utilized.

This picture, in the final analysis, has a balance of two masses: 1) the still life and 2) the foot of the table underneath it.

We find once again the arrangement of the 1922 *Cheminée*. The chimney-piece properly speaking, in its realistic figuration, corresponds to that of the foot of the table, and the Cubist figurations on the still-life are analagous.

I have been insisting, in all the works examined, on the pictorial space and its components, as if I was forgetting Braque's ultimate aim in a picture, which is "poetic creation." I have done so on purpose as the latter would have been revealed as continually the same, under more or less different appearances.

This "poetic creation," so well defined by the painter when he says: "A lemon next to an orange ceases to be a lemon and becomes a fruit, and so does the orange," means that the object painted must lose its utilitarian attributes and express no more than the *idea* of it, which unites its two qualities of a particular object and a significant form, and from which radiates an "aura" of lyrical painting, culminating in a global lyricism which is meaning plus emotion—what one might call an "idea-emotion" or an "emotion-idea," the difference between the two being as follows: in the first case, the idea, originally perceived or understood by "impregnation, obsession and hallucination," is transformed into emotion; in the second, the emotion originally felt, is transformed in the plastic and æsthetic elements of the work and transformed again by "impregnation, obsession and hallucination," beginning with the last (the lyrical *fact* of the emotion), which becomes obsession (what constitutes the emotion), and then impregnation (the æsthetic realization of the object contemplated), and thus returns to the original idea which inspired it. In both cases the idea, the original schema realized by the painting of the picture, is effaced or, better still, merged with and incorporated into the emotion.

Whatever the object in question, it is no longer a guitar, a mandolin, a pot, a fruit-dish, a glass or an apple; it is *the* guitar, *the* mandolin, *the* pot, etc..., the indefinite article in each case being replaced by *the*, which raises the object to its absolute, essential value and gives it its emotional as well as its æsthetic and lyrical power. Braque's "poetic creation" is nothing else but this.

ENRICHMENTS

1929-1931

THE years 1929-1931 produced first of all the *Marine Subjects* at Varengeville, new *Still Lifes* and *Female Heads* (1929); then in 1930 further *Still Lifes*, the *Double Heads* and the first *Baigneuses*, followed in 1931 by more *Baigneuses* and *Still Lifes* which ressemble them, with curving enveloped forms.

It was Paul Nelsons who brought Braque back to Normandy, which he had known since childhood but had abandoned in favor of Sorgues and La Ciotat. The place chosen was Varengeville, near Dieppe, where he built, with Paul Nelsons as architect, the house in which he lives during the summer and part of the fall.

From this year date the first new *Seascapes*. We are confronted with visual space as Braque conceives it: "that which separates objects from each other." To grasp this we must go back to Cézanne.

For Cézanne, landscapes were built up or, more accurately, *woven*, according to a system of parallel planes and lines more or less perpendicular to them, and they were represented in that framework. Then, more and more and right up to his last landscapes, there appeared a dense, physical, overwhelming space, the blue of the Provençal atmosphere, which became predominant and bathed everything.

The visual space in a picture is an atmospheric void between the level of the canvas, that is to say the painter's level, and the level of the spectator, and the background of landscape is painted in. The sky limits the depth of the edge of the horizon. This atmospheric space is thus a form, not because of its content (like the tactile space of the still lifes) but because of its extent, a form in which the sky distributes and apportions the light. Under the sky and on the terrestrial expanse are situated the figurative elements of the landscape, separated by distances and according to successive planes, diverging from each other in various directions, lateral, oblique or in depth. Their separation is the function of this visual space, of the underlying construction, whether stiff or supple, of a perspective, valid only for them and not for the space, which is situated between them and the sky above.

For Cézanne this disposition is that of the country itself, as well as spatial, treated geometrically and constructed strictly on a frame of parallel levels and lines of perspective. The visual space is not a void but an almost material, colored atmosphere—"a place and a connection in depth." The sky does not limit its depth at the horizon because sky and atmosphere make one.   It is not a container for things contained, nor an expanse; it is an *atmospheric density*.   The sky does not distribute an apportioned light, it *is* the colored light infused into the figurative elements of the landscape which make up a connected whole, a land-mass included in the atmospheric mass and barely differentiated from it.   Look at *L'Estaque* in the Musée du Jeu de Paume, Paris, and the series of the *Montagne Ste. Victoire*.   The tones of the objects (houses, trees, mountains, water) are no more than variants of the general blue tonality, variants in which the reds, greens or yellows appear only through the blue.   One might say that in Cézanne's landscapes the "local color," that of the site, is substituted entirely for the individual tones of the figurative elements.   Thus we cannot talk about true visual space but only pictorial space.

For Corot, and Monet or Renoir before Impressionism, Italian perspective is implicit in the picture. Their landscapes are what they see, translated by their sensibility.   The picture's visual space appears in a spatial, atmospheric, empty expanse.   We can see that in the later periods of Monet and Renoir it is no longer the same.   With Monet the individual tone disappears, swallowed up in the composition of the light; we find also, as in Cézanne but differently, the creation of a space purely pictorial.   With Renoir visual space becomes a diffusion in light of the chromatic components of the landscape figuration.   The individual tone of the object does not disappear but is diffused and impregnates space.

What is this *visual space* of Braque?   He has defined it as that which separates objects from each other.   Does it resemble that of Corot, or that of Van Gogh?   No, but it owes something to both.

Between the foreground of the picture and the sky there is nothing dense or apprehensible (which there is in both Corot and Van Gogh), but a void of supreme limpidity and transparency, a fluid without consistency.   The eye, crossing this space, goes to the horizon without any effort in covering the expanse, but *strikes* it in the background, or rather, it comes up against the impassable limit, the limit of the sky, which is material (as in Van Gogh).   This space is certainly a form but not a true container.   It is the form only of its emptiness, and without color.

It is the limit of the sky which closes the visual space.   Sometimes it is somber, tragic, gray-black; a sky to announce the Apocalypse, jostled by clouds of dark green and yellowish gray with gleams of ochre, which recall and even repeat El Greco's tormented flying masses; or it may be of violent azure.   There are skies of great heat or of a storm at sea, pregnant with lightning and the unleashing of the tempest (Pl. 68-72).

It is this sky, the opposite of Corot's, which gives color value and expressive value to the cliffs, the strands, the boats and the sea, a thin dark strip, the horizon being very low.   The light and the colors lit by it are neither in the sky nor in the atmosphere.   They are localized, hard and rough on these cliffs, strands and boats, standing out strongly against the lyrical power of the sky.   It is exactly what one sees after a storm, with all the usual values upset.   The trees, houses, fields, the whole of nature become lighter, in opposition to the thick heavy weight of the sky.   The sky also, curiously enough, recalls the complementary values in the background of Cézanne's still lifes.   It does not participate in the landscape but is the "local color" of the sea, like Cézanne's "local" blue.   It thus creates a visual space, a void to be filled up with objects separated from each other.

The cliffs are successive planes, painted one behind the other, or alternately when there are several of them.   If the plane nearest to us is on the right of the canvas, the next one, further off, is on the left.   All of them leave a gap through which the sea and above it the sky appear on the horizon.   An expanse of space fills in the picture to its very edges.   It becomes vaster, more cosmic.   We must look at it from one side to the other, we are never drawn toward the point of impact of the lines of perspective.   We have thus imposed on us a total visual space which extends imperatively in all directions and obliges us to look at it in its entirety and adjust our eyes to it.

The seascapes, of storm or rain, tend to poetic creation.   Normandy is a region of much rain and the sea in the Channel can be very dangerous.   The cliffs, with a predominant light tonality, which, at Varengeville, Dieppe or Etretat, fall abruptly to the shingle beaches, only attain their intense emotive power under dark skies, while the seascapes only reach tragic grandeur when a storm is threatening.   They are then elevated to the state of a "lyrical object."   The three stages of poetic creation are present: 1) poetic inspiration: the tragedy of the sea; 2) æsthetic realization: the opposition between earth and sky and the total space which gives the measure of its immensity; 3) poetic creation attained: the painting creates an emotive climate through the æsthetic one.

Still Lifes

The still lifes of 1929 continue those studied earlier, with a few new contributions which we shall point out.

In the still life called *Le Journal* (1929; Pl. 60) we may note the newspaper which forms an angle which we know: that of the music scores. One can see in it the idea of future angles, those in *Billiards* for example. The pot is in two zones and is flecked with little horizontal commas, which recall the figurative touches of the pebbles in the pictures of "Marine Objects."

In *The Round Table* at Washington (1929; Pl. 55) it is the angular construction of the planes which is prophetic of work to come. Look at the angle formed by the background wall: it is a forerunner of those in the *Blue Mandolin* of 1930 and the *Red Tablecloth* of 1931, and even more of those in the *Yellow Tablecloth* (1935; Pl. 84) and *Billiards* (1945; Pl. 117).

The *Blue Mandolin* (1930) returns to the *Round Table* and enlarges it, at least by the still life which is in contrary figurations. To the angles it opposes overlapping curves. The table is only indicated by half a drawer. The background of the picture is as important as the still life. The bottom is a juxtaposition of vertical and verticalized planes painted in imitation wood; the top is a wall whose five sections make a corner angle. The tablecloth, with its multiple vertical folds slanting to the left, has a closely spotted pattern which harmonizes with the pseudo-point of the imitation wood.

Braque repeats the theme and transposes it in a painting of 1943 (Pl. 108).

In a number of the still lifes (of 1930 and 1931) there are new figurative elements to be found, allied to those in the *Baigneuses* painted in the same year, either by reproduction or adaptation.

In some there is an opposition of rhythms and the figurations have no other purpose but to objectify the rhythms. The interest lies in the apparition of *curved oblong planes.* Another still life confronts, compensates and balances its curves in a figuration which is neither Cubist nor realist. The reality of the painting is reduced to touches of color round the curved drawing; its space is defined by the wallpaper. A final one (1931), of an extreme violence of figuration, is a "close-up" in which the objects are schematized and rhythmically distorted. The bunch of grapes consists of seven circles on a surface with a quadruple curve in three tones. The glass is checkered like a decorative element. Above is a circle round a sort of ellipse which makes a setting for a flat, vertical curve. Vertical planes are outlined in the background and the whole rests on an oblong curve.

Female Heads

The *Female Heads* are spaced out over the years 1928, 1929 and 1940, and may be grouped according to the two kinds of appearance they present: 1) in double division, 2) in double aspect. The former are of 1929 and the latter of 1929 and 1930.

The heads in double division continue the opposition of light and dark in the fruit dishes, bottles or jugs, but have, in addition, on the dark side, a prolongation of white or near white. (Cf. Pl. 67; Pl. p. 19.)

The dark part takes the form of a very acute angle whose point is at the bottom. In Pl. 67 the features (the chin, the lower jaw up to the ear, the nose, the space between the eyes, the mouth and the eyebrows) are thin white lines with or without an added black one. The hair is of a uniform shade. In the other (1929; Pl. p. 19) we find the same division, the same white drawing of the features, but finer. The hair is in two shades: light in the dark triangle, with white lines indicating the waves; dark in the light part with white lines again for the waves. The background is multiple: a wallpaper with diamond pattern on the right, a thin white strip, the top of the dark angle, another light strip corresponding to the light part of the face which becomes another triangle, with apex at the top, beyond the upper edge of the canvas. Then comes a dark plane. The true tactile space is reserved for the shoulders with their clearly indicated volume.

Heads in double aspect (1929-1930). These are completely detached from reality and attain surrealism. Were Picasso's experiments perhaps responsible for these distortions? The double aspect is not really such except in the 1930 picture where two faces are juxtaposed (Pl. p. 19), the right one higher than the left and the junction effected by a half-mouth which they have in common.

The "Baigneuses"

These may also be divided into two groups: 1) 1930, with Cubist memories; 2) 1930-1931, with curved oblong planes. Although they have no resemblance to Picasso's Dinard pictures (August 1928), it is impossible not to think of these when considering them. The Dinard period is an entirely triangular figuration

of the beach. It has dynamic themes: "the ball game," "entry into the bathing cabin," and an erotic resonance particularly in the "*Baigneuse couchée*" who in addition resembles a crab. In other pictures with the
"ball game" theme, a running female reminds one of an octopus. One of the characteristics of these figures
is the tiny round head at the top of a long neck and the three points which alone suggest the eyes and the
mouth.

Apart from these points, from the long neck, tiny head and a few triangles, and from the assimilation
of a character to a marine animal, one can see hardly any resemblance between Picasso's Dinard period and
Braque's "*Baigneuses.*"

One cannot speak of imitation, and if there is an influence, it lies in refutation, contradiction or, to
say the least, in a different interpretation of the beach. Picasso had synthesized the beach in the triangular
dynamism of the "ball-game," "the game with the dog," the "bathing cabins," and the eroticism of the
"*Baigneuse Couchée,*" whereas Braque concentrates the summer feeling in the sea and the slack recumbent
bodies. There is no eroticism even though there is sensuality. The beach is not a complication of angles
or triangles, but on the contrary gives priority to the curves of the female body.

First paintings of "Baigneuses," 1930. A female stretched on the sand occupies the whole width of
the canvas; she is alone.

In the first we know of, the body is distorted. The breasts are two little half-spheres shaded on the
left; the very small round head is to the left of the thin neck and marked with three points (the eyes and
mouth); the arms make precise angles and a triangle surmounts the belly. On the left are the two angles of
two roofs. The sand includes a square based pyramid on the right. It recalls in its touches of different colors,
the strand at the foot of the *Cliffs* at Varengeville.

A little later, in our opinion, but still of 1930 the *Baigneuse* II (Pl.73) is a variant of the preceding
one, with more curves, except for the angle of the roof on the right and the two arms which are themselves
no more than angles, and which thus rest the head (four points instead of three) on two rectangular planes
also forming an angle between them; the whole figuration is curved. In the background is a vertical shadow-
figure, a half guitar which with its double contours resembles a female body. Under the female is a mat
with a design of parallel waves disposed horizontally.

We may mention a *Baigneuse* III very close to the last but in which the figuration of the beach already announces a *Baigneuse* IV who unlike the others which are nudes, wears curiously enough, a striped bathing costume and even stockings. The cabins are more numerous in the background on the left; three balancing triangles emphasize the displaced hips, more noticeable with her than with the others; she has the shape of a recumbent S.

Braque continued his 1930 experiments but the theme of the recumbent female is isolated from the idea of the beach. The painting (Pl. 74), still in the artist's studio, is situated in an interior. It has been completed after twenty years (1931-1951) and is characterized by the multiplication of spherical surfaces, one covering the other, which are almost concentric toward the left.

The *second paintings of Baigneuses* have two figures, one standing and the other recumbent.

The format of the picture in *Baigneuse* V (Pl. 75) is slightly reduced in width. We may note that (a) the recumbent female makes a half circle. The bust rests on cushions and is almost vertical; the legs are raised, the left crossed over the right and the whole body is in a circle which indicates its contours. The breasts are two little circles and not half-spheres; a large navel centers the stomach between the double inverted curve of the hips; the head is a horizontal oval, double pointed; four spots and a line: two verticals for the eyes, a horizontal line for the nose, and two verticals, again for the mouth. The lifted arms are only slightly indicated in contour. Behind this figure are two houses, one above and in front of the other. (b) The standing figure is behind the other, drawn like it except for the head which is a circle without spots. Its arms stretch out, behind it, a cloth whith horizontal creases. On its left is an almost completely vertical mast which cuts the horizon line at right-angles. The whole picture is thickly painted. (c) The curved oblong superposed planes are those of the still lifes mentioned above. One follows the contour of the recumbent female; the other goes beyond the limits of the standing figure and, following the right arm, thins out and joins the recumbent figure at the level of the left breast. The whole picture is composed of curves, accentuated by the vertical lines of the walls and the mast, the straight lines of the roofs, ascending at an angle and the window-shutters. The verticality of the houses would cause a lack of balance; the bust and raised legs of the recumbent female and the bust of the standing figure participate in the verticality but modified by their curved contours.

The *Baigneuse* VI repeats the same theme with the following variants. (a) The recumbent figure is slightly slanted; the legs and bust are barely raised. In front of her is an open umbrella on the deck-chair on which she is stretched, and behind her are the two houses. (b) The standing female, sketched in curves, comes running with right arm outstretched toward the recumbent female. Behind her is the mast. The sea is represented by a few long, narrow horizontals of stippling. (c) A third figure is seated at the bottom on the right, wearing a jacket with little rectangular spots which repeat, with a variation, the stippling of the sea. (d) The superposed curved, oblong planes are those of the last picture, with the difference that the curve which envelops the raised half-figure, now envelops a whole one. Its form is that of an octopus, which was only potentially so in a previous picture. The X of the deck-chair on which it reposes, is also found in the *Baigneuse* V.

The recumbent figure in *Baigneuse VII : The Beach* (Pl. 76) is a loose curve without true feminine contours. Head and arms are similar. The umbrella is an oval stretching upwards, divided in two by the beginning of a sleeve. The hair is a falling curl. The standing figure is surrounded by a patch of paint in the form of a fish, while in another picture (*Baigneuse VI*) it suggests an octopus. The deck-chair under the recumbent figure is indicated by a flat X. As regards the superposed, oblong, curved planes, there is no change for the recumbent figure, but for the upright one the form is that of a flat fish with a V-shaped tail. Above the stretched out figure is a white curved mass which resembles a plaster bust reduced to an armless trunk and buttocks.

In *Baigneuse VIII* (Pl. 77) (Coll. Walter P. Chrysler Jr.) the rhythmic complexity increases and the components dominate the figuration, even the bodies of the women. (a) The recumbent female recalls that of the last picture except for the head and the legs with raised thighs. (b) The standing female more or less reproduces those in the other pictures. (c) The superposed, oblong, curved planes are as follows: 1) Around the standing figure is the flat fish; 2) In the case of the recumbent figure the plane is practically a half circle and suddenly, with the horizontal head, becomes a crescent moon as popularly conceived with a nose and mouth, in fact a *profile* of the head. Very dark, it is detached in the white oval of the same lunar head, front-face, as indicated by the eye, and by the mouth which is detached, like a little flame from that of the crescent. We may also note: (d) The arms of the recumbent figure are in the shape of a lyre; (e) Another enveloping curve ascends from the shoulder of the recumbent female; (f) Yet another descends from the table toward her belly; (g) The table, which is another superposed curved plane, encircles the tray with two plates and a siphon of seltzer water, seen vertically.   On the round table is an apple, a spiral which unrolls inversely to form a second which prolongs itself and suggests the glass on the second plate, made up of another pseudo-spiral.   This table has replaced the umbrella; (e) Between the table and the enveloping curved plane is a *white* patch in the form of a Romanesque doorway.   What can be the meaning of this patch?   It has a relationship of whiteness with the lunar front-face of the female.   This balancing relationship may perhaps be interpreted as an illusion to a night with full moon, but it can just as well be a simplification of the pseudo-statue in the last picture.

The merging of curves with the very rare rectilinear components, the verticalities indicated at the top of the canvas, give this work a composition both solid and almost paradoxical.   The picture seems to be a half ring starting from the head of the upright character, and ending on the far side at the summit of the lyre made by the arms, in the triangle of the little house.   The struggle for balance between the curved and vertical components is won by the curves.

The "poetic creation" in these works is easily apprehended.   The beach is a place of sensuality and repose, or "relaxation" since the word is fashionable.   It is a muscular relaxation—the contrary of Picasso's Dinard period—expressed by the variety, number and amplitude of the curved lines.   These *baigneuses* are not certain or specific *baigneuses*, but the female body relaxed in summer idleness.   As for the Still Lifes of the year 1931, they are variants, whether allied to the *Baigneuses* or revealing new forms of experimentation.

In one the linear arabesques derive from those of the *Baigneuses* and the table repeats the spirals which we know, giving their forms to two plates, apples and a glass.   It reminds one of the archaic Greek pottery of which Braque has always been so fond.   It is executed in a limited surface analogous to that of a cinema screen, and reminds us of the oval or diamond shaped pictures of 1909.   The glass and fruit dish are in the same sinuous line and between them a sort of treble clef which recalls the hair of the recumbent *baigneuses*.   The grapes are four circles.   We know them too.

In another, *The Red Tablecloth*, the still life properly speaking is made of enveloping curved planes: the body of the guitar, the fruit dish, the plate with two pieces of fruit, the tablecloth, the napkins (one all red and the other with red spots).   This tablecloth is prolonged on to the wall like a double of itself, which is important as we find the prolongation again as a constructive element in the works of 1933 and above all in the *Pink Tablecloth* (Pl. 79).

We may note the *Still Life with Fruit Dish and Napkin*, for it is considered as the first state of the *Pink Tablecloth*.   It includes a fruit dish, a superposed curved plane, a second fruit dish which makes a white circle round the enveloping patch for the fruit, a rolled-up napkin, in the form of a bone because it is also an enveloping curve become an object, and the knife (Pl. 82).

Of the two tablecloths the larger is in the form of a flattened arc; the smaller with white stippling and lobes ascends to the upper edge of the canvas.   That in the form of a flattened arc is a fusion of itself and the pedestal table, as one can divine in it the shape of a drawer.   It is a vast superposed curved plane.   The rhythmic components are all curved even when as in the little tablecloth, they are vertical.

This curved structure is that of the *Pink Tablecloth* of 1933 and reappears in a different form in 1946 in the *Femme au Miroir*.

The period 1929-1931, as we can see, was for Braque one of enrichment by multiple experiments.   If we glance at the work accomplished, we can see in it a perfect continuity carried on by successive contributions, one completing the other and giving it its meaning even when it *seems* to refute it, as it repeats it differently, so as to extract from it a possibility of composition whose final aim is always a double essence indivisibly bound together: plastic and poetic.

This poetic creation remains for him at every moment, the ultimate result of the lyrical conditions called forth.   It is their justification and their culmination in the pictorial fact.   The whole continuity of Braque's work lies in these "experiments with a view to improvement," to quote Mallarmé's definition of his poems.

REFLECTION AND GROWTH
1932-1938

THE year 1932 was not for Braque a year of discoveries. He apparently wished to reflect on his recent work. It was not until 1933 that he felt the necessity of beginning again, and this was also the year when he gave up putting on the paint thin.

Before beginning the period 1932-1938 we may note that in the years 1930-1931 Braque returned to his old favorites, the pre-classical Greek artists and drew in the most archaic manner, using themes of pure fantasy. He also sought inspiration in the paintings on Greek vases and Etruscan mirrors, and he studied the old illustrations and engraving of the 18th century, particularly those on stone, of which he made engraved plasters. The plaster is painted black and on this coating he engraved in white.

Picasso had illustrated Ovid's *Metamorphoses* for Ambroise Vollard, and Braque was asked to illustrate Hesiod's *Theogony*, which did not however appear until 1955.

In 1933 Braque returned to thick paint and began a whole series of still lifes in which the pink already used in preceding years is the predominant tone, with figurations of decorative style in arabesques.

The *Pink Tablecloth* (oil and sand on canvas. 1933; Pl. 79) is the enlargement of another picture, *Still Life with Fruit-Dish and Napkin*, painted in 1932 (Pl. 82). The component curves are practically alone in it, with different variations of superposed curved, oblong planes.

The picture can be divided into two encircling curves: 1) The bottom one with an upward convexity (the flattened arc of the large pink cloth); 2) The top one with a downward convexity which borders the bottom of the still life and which one can, in imagination, continue upwards. It contains the whole still life and the gray central plane of the background edged with carmine.

The still life is inscribed in an ellipse not entirely represented, which begins at the bottom by the plane with the downward convexity. It turns round a pseudo-center which would be the apple in two colors, yellow and rose-violet, placed below the glass. It turns as follows: 1) The fruit-dish, composed of an ascending curved plane and surmounted by a small spherical black and white fruit; 2) The second fruit-dish (another

46

oblong curved plane) with two fruits curving into the right. The return of the circle is not effected by other figurations of objects on the right, but by a black arabesque which goes from the fifth fruit of a third fruit-dish to end up under the music score, passing over the pipe.

If we look attentively at the forms of the object, we must conclude that their roundness and their curves are functionally united. The first fruit-dish, stretching upwards, is compensated, even neutralized in its ascent by the second, whose two superposed apples turn slightly to the right, and whose upward thrust is increased by the three planes above the glass. The third fruit-dish is a curve (yellow and white) whose major axis is parallel to the direction of these three planes. But the arrangement of the five fruits which it holds (2, 2 and 1) forms a sort of point directed downwards; that is to say the axis of the fruit-dish and the axis of the five fruits thus arranged, make an X. This axis of the fruit arrangement begins a descending curve on the right which goes on to continue the arabesque of the fifth fruit.

The music score is slightly slanted so that it follows the encircling curve of the still life.

The glass, with volumes indicated in its schematization, is surrounded by a curved white strip. The fruits are ringed with black.

In the foreground one can make out a sort of hand with three fingers and the beginning of a fourth, the thumb on the left terminated by a little cross into which the arabesque already mentioned comes and includes itself. It passes transparently above the score.

Rhythmic components. They are all curved and yet a number of them can be likened to components in vertical and horizontal directions. 1) The components in vertical directions are the pseudo-hand, the edge of the left-hand fruit-dish, the glass and what surrounds it, the little brown tart, ringed with yellow above the fruit-dish with five fruits, the two apples of the second fruit-dish (with what surrounds them), the gray curved plane of the cloth which, behind the top of the still life, goes as far as the upper edge of the canvas, and the triangles at the bottom of the cloth. 2) The components in horizontal directions are the projections of the score, the fruit-dish with five fruits and the fruits themselves, the X which they form, being resolved by the bisection on the horizontal line; the upper curve of the cloth, the projection on the right of the second fruit-dish, the bottom of the cloth, the top of the first fruit-dish, the reddish-brown triangles on the right of the gray cloth, and finally the pipe. 3) Mixed components are the involuted edges of the gray cloth with white stippling and horizontal blacks, the first fruit-dish in its lower part, the black tracing ringed with yellow of the pseudo-hand, and the two red planes on each side of the ascending gray. 4) The encircling oblong curved planes consist of all the figurations except the score, the fruit, pipe and glass being adaptations of oblong, curved planes. Here they are encircling, not superposed.

Space. 1) Visual space: This is absent, there being no true background because the background is entirely participant, its curves merging with all the others. 2) Tactile space: This is predominant; each object is placed so that it gives the illusion of being touchable in a limited, carefully constructed space. 3) Total space: Braque has realized this by the merging of tactile space with visual space.

The work is at the same time both deep and level. The foreground (the pseudo-hand) is not separable from the ascending gray plane of the background. It implies the level of the canvas but is not necessarily on it like the rectangular plane of the "*Grande Cheminée.*"

To appreciate the importance of the encircling curved planes, one has only to look at the sanguine, *The Apples* (Pl. 81), a study (0.50 × 0.76) for a painting (0.89 × 1.16) in the Walter P. Chrysler Jr. Collection. Though not figurative here, the winding round the center situated by the apples recalls in a surprising way that of the *Baigneuse VIII* round the pedestal table of the second plane (Pl. 77).

The Yellow Tablecloth (1935; Pl. 84) is equally celebrated but very different from *The Pink Tablecloth*, of which it is almost the contrary since visual space is predominant, constructed as it is by the walls of the room making a deep angle in which, as in the middle, the table with its divergent lateral edges, is isolated. Everything is in oblique lines creating angles. The only curved lines present are in the still life properly speaking: the basket, the slanting fruit, the bottle and the guitar, distorted into a quasi-arabesque plane.

The verticality of the work is strongly marked, but all the slanting or directive lines and the multiple curves of the still life, compose it without diminishing it. It is an absolute balance but profoundly paradoxical as each representative element which constitutes it is in itself an unreality culminating in a plastic super-reality whose final result is a poetic "operation," or, if you like, a poetic creation by means of the magic

which Braque defines thus: "Magic is the sum of the means which excite credulity," and again "Magic is no less dangerous for the one who uses it than for the one who experiences it."

In *The Mandolin* (1936; Pl. 88) the decorative elements dominate and the work is constructed as a theme of curved rhythms framed in a web-work of rhythmic verticals and horizontals.

The centers of attraction and balance (I mean the object which most draws the eye and the center of gravity of the composition) are superimposed in the body or sound box of the mandolin. There are very few objects: the mandolin, the score, a pipe and a glass. They are on a table. The plastic complexity of the table components is extreme, their planes being those of synthetic Cubism. The table has at the same time a square top and a round top. The square top (visible particularly on the left) is the *real* one. The round top, which cannot be assimilated to a cloth, is the *support* of the still-life whose curved lines it reinforces. The glass also yields to the attraction of the curve and is distorted toward the right.

Components. The vertical and horizontal components frame the still life to emphasize its curving development. 1) The vertical components consist of the whole background wall, the verticality of the glass, the bowl of the pipe, the left lateral edge of the table and the lines of the planes which frame the still life. 2) The horizontal components are the frieze of the background wall on the right, the designs of the wood of the square table, the near edge of this table and the upper edge of the plane which frames the top of the still life. 3) The oblique components are reserved for the planes situated under the still life. Their role is to pass from the vertical or horizontal planes to the curves of the still life, being both linear (in the axes of the slant) and level (on the surface of the planes). The equilibrium of the work is attained by a total immobility.

Colors. The strongest contrasts are reserved for the still life, as it is the spectacular theme of the work and the directive theme of the composition. The framing planes are also contrasted but with less violence as they have no other role but to establish and participate. They are the complementary themes.

48

SCULPTURES

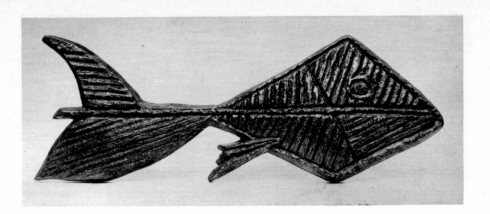

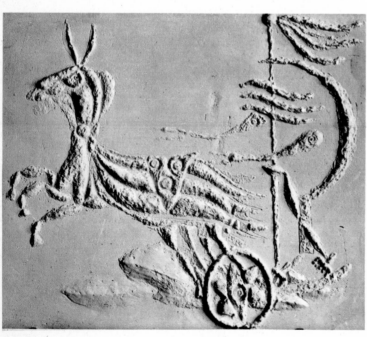

The pictures which follow, the "figures," are another stage in Braque's work, and one studded with masterpieces.

The *Woman at an Easel* (1936. Pl. 90), though it is not the first attempt at a double visage (we studied this in the *Female Heads* and even more in the last of the *Baigneuses* with the lunar face), is the first picture in which the double visage enters into the essential structure of the work, as the duality is so effected as to organize it by spatial oppositions in a light-dark contrast.

We may recall that in the last of the *Baigneuses*, the recumbent female had a face composed of a dark crescent moon included in a round full-face, the two aspects united by the lips of the mouth. We find this division once more in the *Woman at an Easel*. The left part is dark and seen in profile; the right is full-face for the face and neck, and three-quarter face for the bust. This right part is a light shade.

The light-dark contrast is present throughout the picture, which is divided into three vertical planes of equal surface. 1) On the right is a dark plane in which is inscribed a black and white easel, a pot in two shades and a palette. 2) In the center is a decorative background with a chain motif (circles and diamonds) in a light shade. 3) On the left we find the same motif slightly darker. At the bottom is part of a pedestal. The balance is obtained by the two lateral planes: the dark wall and the easel which compensates the black profile of the feminine figure opposite to it. Between them is the light part of the figure under the light plane of the wall.

Component framework. It is very rigid as it consists of vertical components, this picture being only conceived vertically, in the three background planes, the easel, the pot with the two curves of the palette and the black profile. The horizontal components are reduced to the pedestal at the bottom left, the line of the eyes and mouth, and the square neck of the dress. The oblique components of the easel make an angle, while the background "diamonds" accentuate the vertical components.

Space. This is neither tactile nor visual; one might call it *visuo-tactile.* The black profile implies a situating plane for the figure near the real level of the canvas. The front view situates it both behind the profile of the face and neck, and in front of the profile of the bust by an indication, vague though it be, of the outline of breasts under the corsage. The palette is on the level of the canvas, the pot is behind it, and behind that again, the easel. There is no true visual space because there is no true depth. The angle constructed by the easel envelops the figure and foreshortens the depth. There is no true tactile space either as the objects are not separated, either from each other or from us. There is however, a superposition of planes: the palette, then the pot, then the female figure in front of the easel, but they are not touchable at an imaginable distance. Only the spatial plenitude is valid, as that only is sought. The figurations seem to have been constructed only as an "inventory" of plastic elements, culminating in the total spectacle of a space not divisible into volumes, as they are only suggested by approximations. This very particular construction, only sketched here, is enlarged, complicated and multiplied in the succeeding pictures.

Woman with Mandolin (1937; Pl. 89). There are no longer three vertical planes in the background, but two, separated by a black line. Each in its turn is divided into two: a dark part against the edge of the picture and a light part in the center. Though this center part is certainly light, its role is not to diffuse light. It happens to be the best lighted part.

Rhythmically all the components are vertical. The space is decidedly visual as one notices a depth indicated by the checkered carpeting on the floor and the distances which separate from the background both the figure and the column with the score on it. But it is also a total space because it is limited and without any possible extension, even imaginary, in any direction.

This totality is made denser by the choice of colors, multiply dispersed, which react on each other, being respectively more somber or more strident (though still restrained). Yellows, ochres, mauves, violets and grays are opposed to greens, oranges, pinks and a few browns and blacks. Some of the colors stand out like gleams of light.

The Painter's Studio (1939; Pl. 92). It is divided into two by the easel. The background has two constituents: 1) a large irregular pentagon whose right part is light, almost violently so; 2) the right of the background which is almost dark. The pentagon is framed by the darkest tonalities in the work. It completely surrounds the painter, the easel and the model.

Figures. 1) The painter. He is sitting in an armchair, palette in hand, has long hair, a pointed beard, and smokes a cigarette. He looks at the model and is himself painted in two zones, light and dark. The chair continues the two zones and over-runs the encircling pentagon by its decorated planes. The features are drawn on the black of the dark zone. 2) The model is a female nude with the double visage, familiar to us. The light part is much the most important. The contours of the body, drawn like those in the *Canephorae*, are in white lines, except the eye which is in brown ones. The falling hair is auburn and the legs are covered by drapery. The dark part is a profile for the face. The arms and the slope of the body continue the front-face of the light part. Behind the head and over-running the pentagon is a black and white mirror. 3) The easel. It is in the form of a lyre and painted in imitation wood. It occupies the center of the picture and carries a small canvas on which one can see the model, drawn in white.

Rhythmic development. The painter, his easel and the nude model are placed slantwise. The painter is on the level of the canvas and the model behind, with the easel half-way. He is in two zones, the lighter toward the lateral edge of the canvas, the darker toward the center, which it reaches with the legs, the chair and the palette. The model is also in two zones, the dark toward the edge of the canvas, and the light toward the center, that is to say inversely to the painter.

Components. The verticals predominate, whether constituted by the figures, the easel, the wallpaper or the chair. The horizontals do no more than compensate, attenuate and establish. The curves are presented by the model and, to balance them, the back of the painter's chair. In the center is the palette and the two upper lateral extremities of the easel, in the shape of a lyre.

This picture recalls practically all Braque's earlier work, after Cubism. The encircling pentagon is an adaptation of the pictures in oval framing, or the cinema screen type. The figures are either double or in black profile like the *Mandolin Player*. The wallpapers participate and radiate.

The light slants from the front to the back and from left to right and, thus directed, permits all the light-dark contrast.

Space. It is multivalent, associating visual space and tactile space to make a univalent poetic creation; a total space, not dense but made up of relations between the figurations and the background.

With this *Studio*, Braque exhausted all the possibilities offered to him by the theme which one might call "Figures in Composition."

The "poetic creation" is the *ambiance*, the atmosphere, or if you like, transposing the well-known phrase applied to landscapes, giving it other resonances, "a state of mind." This poetic creation is the state of artistic intimacy, the lyricism in the salon of a painter or a musician. The denseness or unified multiplicity of the space in a studio or a salon is a denseness of impregnation. The idea effaces itself, to leave only the lyric value of the poetic creation, which one can only apprehend by contemplating it.

What conclusions do we come to concerning these years 1932-1938? Certainly to an enrichment. All the still lifes of this period are exclusively Braque's, but one can find in them figurations dear to other painters of Cubist origin. Braque has treated them with so powerful a personality that one can distinguish them at first glance without needing to look for the signature.

It is a great deal, but as such, Braque would be no more than the greatest of Cubist painters after *his* Cubism had evolved. And it is not enough, we must look for something else in the work of these years, something completely new. His "Figures in Composition" give it to us as well as the *Pink Tablecloth* and the *Yellow Tablecoth*, the former being the first complete realization of a total space. We shall come across others but only the *Femme au Miroir* of 1946 repeats this presentation. The *Yellow Tablecloth* is a combination of tactile space and visual space to create a pictorial space. The "Figures in Composition" construct another kind of total space which includes tactile space.

FURTHER REFLECTIONS
1939-1945

I HAVE observed before that Braque evolves by beginning again. In 1938, spending the summer in Varengeville, he painted a new series of *Cliffs*. The one we reproduce (Pl. 72) decidedly complicates the problem of visual space. There are two cliffs face to face and between them opens the horizon of the sea. The right hand cliff is in three tones: yellow, gray and green. The left hand one is gray-black with yellow gleams, and with "near blacks" for the two walls, one vertical, the other slanting. The strand is gray-blue, as are the two central boats, except the side of the middle one, which is light yellow, with black hull, mast and oar; its sail is gray-white. The boat on the left is black, with a brown gang-plank and light-yellow water line; the mast of the sail is black and brown. In the foreground is the triangular bow of a fourth boat. The sea is dark gray and the whole sky, of a gray-blue, recalls the tonalities of the strand. Finally there are brownish clouds.

The visual space is in four distances: 1) from the level of the canvas to the boat on the left; 2) from this boat to the plane of the cliffs; 3) from the cliffs to the sea; 4) from the sea's edge to the sky background.

The work gives the impression of a seascape after a storm, when the light strikes on certain points and makes them brighter than the sky.

We may note rapidly the nature of a few pictures of these years, 1939-1941, chosen from the still lifes.

The Glass of Wine (1939; Pl. 100) is of extremely simple figuration. It is a close-up. On the left is the half-full glass, the same as that of the preceding still life, and a bunch of grapes with a few black-ringed grapes on a vine leaf with a long stalk. There is a cloth with two stripes and a rolled-up napkin in which one finds the "spiral" again. The tactile space is alone in the picture.

In *Flowers and Palette* (1939; Pl. 110), the plastic composition reveals itself on the contrary as one of the most complicated conceived by Braque. The planes are juxtaposed in all directions. The components are broken up, continued again and inverted. The color values make use of all their possibilities of variation and contrast. Why all this? we may ask. Because "the ultimate aim of a picture is a total space, full, without a void and without directive dimensions." To attain it Braque used everything he had already done, including Cubist fragmentation.

The Studio (1939; Pl. 95), a picture belonging to M. Paul Rosenberg, presents a figurative complication almost as great but more ordered than the preceding one. In contains an easel, a stool, a round table with a palette and brushes, a little table with a vase of flowers, and a wall with a window. Imitation wood, wallpaper, floral arabesques, festoons, hard planes and the straw top of the stool, all combine in a decorative whole, with planes in a vertical direction. The whole attains a total space in which only the visual component (the distance to the plane of the wall) is constructed, not for its own sake but to increase the totality sought for.

We shall speak again, from another view-point, about the *Vanitas* of 1939 (Pl. 97), which is a skull on a suggested table, with next to it a cross and the beads of a rosary. It is a tragic painting, with dull tones and thickly applied paint in which browns and greens dominate. The skull is gray with white lights and there are four vertical strokes on the left hand side of the wall, above the cross and the rosary, which balance the skull. There are at least six versions of this, either of the period, or later or even of the present day. One of these variants, *Jug and Skull* (Pl. 96; 1943), leads us to two very striking little pictures.

We will mention first that of 1940, *Bread*. Daily bread, with the oncome of war, became a reality which took everyone back to the days of the Gospel. For Braque, it is a very simple beautiful picture, a canvas in width, whose two top components, vertical and horizontal, are strongly established by the brown and yellow background wall. The table, yellow-brown broken by black, is seen slantwise. The gray cloth and the yellow-brown bread are oblong curved planes. There are two straw-yellow apples on the right, a black glass with touches of pink and a knife (green blade, brown handle). We shall find the disposition of the walls again in the *Fish* of 1942.

Pitcher and Bread of 1941, in the same spirit, has also a simple subject. There is a loaf of bread, a curved level, which is a replica of that of the preceding picture but inversely situated. There are also two figs, a glass and a jug, and between the bread and the jug, a bunch of grapes, stylized to a maximum degree (round patches, little curved lines). Except for the glass the whole still life is on a napkin with three folds (a curved plane, the smallest fold going upwards). Underneath is a table cover with four folds with ornate borders. The background wall is dark and indicates two vertical strips. The horizontal components are predominant. Space is entirely tactile.

These three years of reflection resulted for Braque in the return to a near-reality and also in the desire to construct a total pictorial space.

Several pictures of these years confirm his return to realism. It was a necessity for him. He drew a new power from the reality of the object, by communion with this reality by which he became impregnated in order to transpose it. All that he had asked up till now from the usual objects or from particular ones (musical instruments, music score), he now asked from objects of domestic or other uses, in which he discovered the possibility of new poetic creation.

The rest he had taken while he was seeking always for a total pictorial space, led him to simplification and to a sort of contemplative humility in front of the modest reality of every day objects. He felt in them a power to be drawn on, not only for their appearance but for their effect of reducing the diversity of his palette to a few very simple colors with variations. This simplicity continued up to 1942.

Having undertaken the pursuit of a total pictorial space, little by little, in work after work, he constructed it as he conceived it and drew near its final plenitude by dint of ever renewed approaches.

In *Flowers and Palette* it is by the almost inextricable juxtaposition of the elements of small surfaces that he wished to create it. This road he knew was the right road and the only road, but he also knew that the multitudinous figurations and rhythms were still an obstacle to be overcome as they brought dispersion, while the solution must be found in cohesion, in the *articulation* of large simple elements. He was to attain it in 1946 with the *Femme au Miroir*, but there are several noteworthy stages in this period: *Interior with Palette* (Pl. 110), *The Blue Guitar* (Pl. 108), *The Green Tablecloths*, and *Billiards* (Pl. 113 and 117).

The 1942 *still lifes.*

In a whole group of still lifes, *Fish and Black Jug, Black Fish, Brown Fish, Three Lemons, Cup and Bunch of Grapes*, the number of objects is reduced to a minimum, three in the *Lemons* and even two in the *Cup and Bunch of Grapes*. Braque found them sufficient to organize the very simple economy of each of these works. He concentrates on them the spectacular figuration and the equilibrating masses. He also reduces the chromatic components to a minimum.

In *Fish and Black Jug*, we find greens, browns, blues, a rose-white and black; in *Black Fish* (Pl. 101) a predominant black, yellows and grays. In *Brown Fish* (the pendant to this in the Musée d'Art Moderne, also called *The Carafe*), black, ochres, grays, two greens and a red brown (for the fish). In *Three Lemons* (Pl. 98) the dominant tone is brown, to which is added blues, a few rare whites, grays, a pinkish brown and an ochre *brisé*. In the *Cup and Bunch of Grapes*, the purple grapes are on a pale green vine-leaf, a gray-black fork is placed horizontally, the cup is in gray-yellows and browns and finally three are two yellows, pale for the table and ochre for the wall.

The spatial disposition of the objects is almost invariably on a slant, as the wall backgrounds are in pronounced vertical and horizontal lines. The table and fish follow an ascending line from left to right in *Black Fish* and inversely in the *Brown Fish*.

In *Three Lemons*, the table is broken up, making a sort of recumbent half X. It ascends from the left as far as the break, and from there comes down again, thus uniting the inverse slanting lines of the *Black Fish* and the *Brown Fish*. There are accordingly two orientations. The figuration rests on the lower angle of the painting, forming an angle which is perhaps a sketch for that found later in *Billiards*, *The Green Table* or *The Terrace* (1950). The general disposition is that of the top of an open fan. The coffee pot in three tones, which also widens upwards, finishes off this opening. The cloth is nothing else but a superposed oblong plane, with its two upper corners encircling the two lemons on the right. The general rhythm is horizontal; all the verticals are slanting and the still life, apart from the lemons, has a level figuration.

The other still lifes of 1942 have different kinds of figuration or presentation.

In the *Red Table* (1942; Pl. 102) it is the décor, the surroundings which count. The still life, reduced to a mandolin, a score and a glass, has spectacular values but is not the motif of the picture. Any other objects presented and constructed in the same way could have replaced them. The picture is a large plane with almost symmetrical dashes of color in which red predominates (the cloth and the background). The other tones, browns, white and a few blacks, give intensity to the reds which vary from the pink of the cloth to the almost vermilion of the background. To be exact, it is a question of a space level which seeks its totality in figuration without depth.

The *Interior with Palette* (1942; Pl. 110), which marks another step in the pursuit of total space, continues in many points, such as the curved planes merging with the other planes, the acquisitions of the *Pink Tablecloth* and prepares the future merging of all planes in the *Femme au Miroir* of 1946. The browns predominate becoming almost black in the curved plane on the right. There are a few true greens (the chair), which superimposed on the browns, make a more or less gray-green. There are also pinkish-grays, the pot and its plant and the fragments of tablecloth near the palette. The richness in color variations is marvellous and makes this picture one of Braque's masterpieces.

57

In the following pictures there is a sort of brusque mutation. It is no longer a question of seeking a true total space but a full tactile space to which the background windows add a fragmentary visual space. It is this last which gives to the still lifes which construct the tactile space, both their spectacular plenitude and their intimate character of every day objects.

I shall limit myself to a few comments. I shall not describe the pictures as they are too well-known and frequently reproduced; the *Toilette Bleue* (Pl. 106), the two versions of the *Toilette devant la fenêtre* (Pl. 109) and the *Femme à la Toilette* (Pl. 103).

The *Toilette Bleue* is tactile space with horizontal components. The three others have vertical components. If there is a great simplicity of composition in the *Toilette Bleue*, the complexity, even though not apparent, in the *Toilette devant la fenêtre* is extraordinary.

The *Femme à la Toilette* on the other hand almost approaches asceticism. The pink-fleshed body is constructed in a mass, with the pink soap on the right and the blue basin with its surrounding browns. The window, a theme which appears more and more in Braque's work, shows a slightly cloudy sky and is here no more than a background, but both spatial and radiating as it increases the intimacy of the scene in this little corner of the room.

In the *Kitchen Table* (Pl. 114) we return to the vertical picture. The framework is vertical with a few horizontal lines in the center and slightly below it: the two red fishes in the pan, the leek and the cupboard. We may note, as we shall find it again, the dark red jug painted in very thick materials. We shall find both materials and color again also.

The Figures

I should like to consider particularly now an essential work of 1942, *Patience* (Pl. 105), as it is no doubt the most totally and poetically beautiful of Braque's creations.

It is a work which is troubling both from the plastic point of view and in its super-poetic meaning. For, as in the *Woman with Marine Background* (Pl. 104) we can distinguish two forms of poetic creation; one is the super-reality of the figuration and the other the super-reality of the meaning.

I. *The Super-Reality of the Figuration.* The work is entirely vertical; all the figurative and decorative lines are ascendants, as well as the chromatic tones and planes. The few rare horizontals are no more than indications to enhance the others by contrast.

Chromatic complexity. This is very great, not so much by the number of the colors but by their multiple variations and mergings, as for example the rose-violet of the table becoming here and there a somber brown; green turning from the yellow-green of the stool with the chess-board, into more or less dark gray-greens, or the blue of the wallpaper with its black design which becomes gray. The grays apart from these have splashes of other colors. There are very few blacks; the woman's profile, a thin tall plane above the chess-board, the plane above the table and those of the chair are tinged with brown.

The patience-player. She is curiously constructed, almost entirely front-face for the body and in profile for the face itself. Participating in the verticality of the work, the bust is distorted upwards. The arm which holds up the head under the chin is like a thin column. The other one, in black, descends in spiral curls of less and less width, becomes narrow before the elbow and turns at a right-angle to make the forearm and the emaciated hand with its very long nails.

The face in profile is not a plane, as it is in the figures of the other pictures. It is modeled from front to back; the profiles of nose and chin are planes in depth; the cheek, the eyes and the black hair with blue lights are curved. Beneath them the neck is a narrow and very slanting plane.

The front view of the face is a plane but the neck which follows it is shaded. The two faces are joined by the mouth which they have in common.

The table, in a shade of violet, is narrow and long with a cover falling very low, like a kind of little coffin. On it are six playing cards and at the end in gray, a bottle of sherry.

Apart from the profile of the figure, the front view of the face and the arm-column, and apart also from the stool with the chess-board, the blue plane and the table with its clearly pronounced line and color, all the rest of the canvas is sort of intense vibration of juxtaposed colors. Exception made of the blacks and the blue on the vertical plane, none of the tones are pure. They all make use of their possibilities of increase or attenuation by immixture and also by brusque proximity. The whole, indescribable as it is, is a multiplicity of elements never before attained by Braque.

The result of this complexity is the creation of a dense space with interconnected parts contained in a container which undoubtedly has depth. For the line of vision, which can be situated very high up on the level of the eyes in the figure, necessitates a downward view on to the chess-board, the table, the figure and the ground, whose carpet and parquetry are sketched in against the woman's chair. But this downward view foreshortens the space. The background wall, very near, limits it, with however the addition that above the head of the player, there are curtain embroideries. The whole left part of the background is a transparent white curtain. The spots of color with which it is strewn come through from the wall behind. Between this curtain on the left and the right-hand part of the background is an entirely blue-black plane. Is it the night? If so, the depth inspired by the table is continued by the night *ad infinitum*.

II. *The super-reality of meaning.* It is included in the super-reality of the figuration and transcends it. It is true that the level of appearance contains the level of meaning, it creates it, but the relations which unite them are no longer only formal; they have a meaning over and above which is no longer only of a plastic order. This super-reality of meaning is to be found in two elements, the figuration of the woman and the window open on the night.

What is the woman doing? Is she actually playing patience? No. Is she thinking? Not even that; she is dreaming and it is her dream, her reverie that separates her from her surroundings. What she looks at, what she follows with her soul's vision, is an obsession of a tragic or at least a dramatic nature. Look carefully at the double visage. Although formally in two figurations, front-face and profile, like those in the *Figures in Composition*, it is different from them because, both in profile and front-face, it means something, it has an expression, which is the same in both aspects.

The profile, by the surface relief which gives it reality, is that of one in pursuit of a dream; the front-face, which consists linearly of prominent cheek bones, a hollow cheek, and a vacant eye, unless it be turned inwards, betoken an overwhelming obsession.

The whole body, which has pivoted at an angle of 90°, is the body demanded by the face. The disproportionate arm-column, the emaciated black arm and the skeleton hand indicate an almost morbid melancholy. The long, narrow table like a coffin, the sherry bottle (is she perhaps a drunkard?) add to the tragedy of the figure. Haunted by her misfortune either past or to come, she has shut herself up in loneliness and desolation.

If the large black plane between the curtains really represents night, then her dream is surely the terrible anguish of a sleepless night when dreams, memories and even projects are so many forms of giddyness and discomfort.

In the preceding *Figures in Composition* as in the *Woman with Marine Background*, I discerned a sort of closed-in atmosphere, either of the intimate moments of the artist in one case, or an illustration of the deadly feminine attraction of a siren in the other. In *Patience*, I find an atmosphere of despair. This woman who plays games of patience, or reads her fortune in the cards, this woman, ridden and hallucinated by misfortune, who seems to be waiting for something. Perhaps even the worst and has nothing to hope for but a miracle, might she not be the image of a woman in the war years of 1939-1944? She is alone, she has perhaps her husband, her son or a beloved who has disappeared and is either dead, a prisoner or perhaps deported. Tomorrow, like today, will be a *night* filled with dire presentiments. She seeks an answer to her question and finds only one and always the same: she must *wait*.

I may be wrong and I did not care to ask the painter himself. The picture may after all be no more than a plastic poetic creation. But even if erroneous, the interpretation I propose would but confirm the magnificence of the work which suggests it.

From "The Coffee Mill" to "Billiards."

If the year 1942 was a fertile one for Braque, one can say as much for the years 1943-1945. The painter returns to what he has already done and seeks to do better. I have made a deliberate choice in the works which stand out in this period, to show the enrichment which took place between *The Coffee Mill* and the painting *Billiards*. Under different appearances, the ultimate aim remains the same: a technique resulting in a pictorial space and a poetic creation.

The Coffee Mill and the Fish (1943; Pl. 107). This is a still life in which a triangle added as partial figuration to the other components of the painting gives it its particular aspect.

What one sees is as follows: a table covered with a cloth; on the cloth a plate with a large fish, a bowl, an onion and a coffee mill. Like all the others this still life is in three planes: 1) that of the onion, 2) that of the fish and its plate, 3) that of the coffee mill. The vertical and horizontal components are equal.

Vertical components. They are divisible into three zones : 1) the right part, limited by a vertical line ascending from the cloth to the middle of the fish and continuing above, on to the wall by means of the framing; 2) the central part, which goes from this line to that which, on the left, cuts the cloth, crosses the coffee mill and ends on the background wall; 3) all the left part. The vertical components are accentuated by the triangles indicated on the bottom of the cloth, by the division of the floor on the right, by the black bottle behind the coffee mill and by the left lateral edge of the cloth. The onion, slightly slanted, must be considered as a vertical component.

Horizontal components. They consist of the inner edge of the table, the gray lines on the triangles at the bottom of the cloth, the fish and its plate, and the top, bottom and handle of the coffee mill; also the triangles of the floor, both on the right and on the left, and the zig-zagging triangles of the background.

Curved components. They are implied in the preceding ones whose directions they follow.

Colors. They are not numerous but multiple in their variations. 1) The brown of the wall is in four tones, from black-brown to pinkish-brown. It continues the same or ends up in black on each side of the table, on the floor. The fish is black-brown, the coffee mill red-brown, the onion touched with orange-brown, the triangles of the cloth and its vertical plane on the right, black-brown. The bottle is almost black. 2) The yellow is reserved for the cloth where it varies from a green-yellow to gray-yellows. It frames the coffee mill and all its figurative elements. 3) The green starts as a gray-green (vertical plane of the cloth where it falls to the left) goes on to the grayish-greens of the handle of the coffee mill and the skin of the onion to become a gray in two tones in the plate with the fish. 4) The grays participate in all the colors. 5) The blacks are very rare and dominated by browns. 6) The white is a pure color around the fish's eye, otherwise (in the onion, the coffee mill etc.) it is pale yellow.

The picture is a dark mass organized around the light mass of the yellow cloth and the onion.

Space. This is tactile (since it is a still life) but entirely implied in a space filled up by the wall and floor, which at the same time push it forward and maintain it as it is. The forward projection is effected by the violent contrast between the light yellows of the cloth and the dark tones around it. We arrive at a total space by the interdependence of these elements, which are equally tactile and visual.

The Green Cover (1943; Pl. 113) and its numerous variants are a return to a shallow space in a close-up. The background has a capital importance because of the thickness of the painting material. Moreover the rhythmic composition is new or at least renewed since the Cubist period with its spider-web background. It diverges from a point in the center of the still life, a divergence clearly indicated by the angles of the top of the table. Only the bowl and the pot of flowers are situated in a horizontal line. The same rhythmic theme appears with variants in other pictures of this year 1943.

Jug and Skull (1943; Pl. 96). Its appearance is that of the several "Vanitas" versions of 1939 and yet it differs from them a lot, in being less somber and less tragic. The skull and the cross have the same shades of color, yellow-white to gray-blue. The skull, cross and jug as well as a kind of cubic lantern under the skull, are on a round table with chromatic variations from multiple browns to grays touched with greens.

We should remark the pitcher. The body of it is painted thickly, in a two-tone material, black-brown on the right and left, and red in the center. This mass, strongly projected by its material thickness, has to be balanced and it is so by the two thick vertical lines and the whites of the cross, the skull and the lantern.

In *Vanitas* the cross and the wooden rosary were already presented in this thick material. They are replaced here by an object of use, the jug. What meaning should we give to this change? If we choose literary associations they would be Shakespearian: the skull of "Poor Yorick." A skull, a cross and part of a rosary. But Vanity is essentially a theme of Ecclesiastes, a classical one in painting; union with God is obtained by solitude and prayer, the contemplation of death and meditation on our last moments. The life of man is but a passage to life eternal.

Vase and Skull (it would be better called "*Jug and Skull*"), while it presents our last moments as the goal, proposes life itself as the means of reaching it. It is the jug which has this significance, of an austere life turned entirely toward a spiritual ideal; the life of prayer, drinking water only, and considering as vain the nourishment of the earth, the only good being in the ascetic nourishment of the soul.

Space. The tactile space is valid for the whole picture. Lantern, cross and jug are separable by "touch." The jug has in addition a tactile material volume, a light between two shades.

60

With *The Salon* (1944; Pl. 112) the theme of the open window reappears in Braque's work. It gives this picture its "inwoven" components as it is entirely organized between straight lines (vertical and horizontal), and curved lines.

The background imposes a rigid verticality which neither the horizontal hand-rail, the separation in two of the window-pane nor the symmetric curves of the balcony, diminish. Under the window only the horizontal lines are shown, because it is actually like this in the room and because they add to the horizontal character of the black table top and strike against the verticality of the little table with a gray-mauve diamond pattern.

With the scattered still life: brown vase on the table, gray flower pot, small brown pot, glass, drawing boards, etc., on the table or near it, other vertical components are inserted in the planes with horizontal direction.

Although in appearance and structure this picture is different and even the opposite from the *Interior at Nice* of Matisse (painted in 1927), it reminds me of it each time I see a reproduction, though not each time I analyze it again. The essence of *The Salon*, as a painting, is not that of the *Interior at Nice*. *The Salon* is a composition of pure painting only. The other is a composition in paint but with poetic "anecdote." Apart from the black and blue and the chestnut of the pedestal which occupy exactly opposite surfaces in the two works, they cannot be compared in chromatic organization as they are regulated by different aesthetic principles.

All the components of *The Stove* (1944; Pl. 111) are vertical. The picture is divided into two : on the left a light part with the yellow walls, the gray stove and the bluish pail; on the right a dark part rather brutally lighted by the strident cadmium of the paper basket, a stridency which compensates for the luminosity of the yellow wall. The carpet is a deep blue with touches of carmine. The palette of yellowish-gray is another light patch compensating for the top of the stove.

The four pictures which follow belong to a period which one might call "yellow"; a golden yellow, the yellow of sunflowers. They are as follows: *The Sunflowers* and *The Red Fish on a Plate* of 1943, *The Grapes on a Plate* and *The Grapes and Jug* of 1944, and in 1946 further *Sunflowers*.

These pictures have a fulgurating violence of presentation, with yellows alone predominant. If we look at *The Sunflowers* (pl. 115-116) or if, knowing them, we try to imagine the components of the three others mentioned above—not the spatial or volumetric ones which, except for those of the tactile space, are secondary—we are forced to submit to the powerful will of the painter. The golden yellow admits no accessory colors but those which participate in or enhance its violence.

In *The Sunflowers* the greens and browns are either true (as in the leaves) or green yellows and a few blacks. In the *Red Fish on a Plate* we find the reds of the fish, ringed with blue, the gray brown of the plate and the browns of the goblets. The *Grapes and Jug* opposes blacks (tinged with brown or green) and the pale yellows of the bunch of grapes and lemon to the reddish table and the pure yellow of the background.

The *Grapes on a Plate* is made up entirely of three tones: 1) the yellow sunflower; 2) the light browns of the plate, the sketch of the glass and the knife; 3) the pale yellow of the grapes.

Braque did not forget these luminous yellows; they participate, partially, in works such as *La Toilette aux Carreaux Verts* (1945) and the *Slice of Pumpkin* (1944).

The Sickle and *The Pumpkin* (1944; Pl. 120 and 121) are two pictures of which one is a pendant to the other in character and composition, the presentation being reversed. In one the jug is on the left, and the sickle continues in a contrary direction the curve of the slice of pumpkin. They have both the same characteristics of harmonized discords.

The Sickle. The jug is rose-violet on the right and red-brown on the left. It is separated by a white line which also frames the outer contour. The sickle is gray-green, its handle red-brown, rather darker than that of the jug. It is isolated by white lines like the jug. The plate on which it is set is of a very similar gray but with brown and greenish variations, and is ringed with white which gets darker toward the jug.

The table is the same in both pictures and in each a chain is hanging from the wall, but it is less important in *The Pumpkin* than in *The Sickle*. The backgrounds are also the same and the space is constructed in exactly the same way.

In both these pictures Braque used daring juxtapositions of colors which, attempted by any other painter (except Matisse or Picasso), would have been jarring. Matisse would have succeeded by dispersing them, Picasso by modulating them. Braque uses an artifice; he separates them by "silences" created by the white contours encircling the objects. The thick powerful texture of the background emphasizes and projects forward the objects of the still life which are painted smoothly.

The Pumpkin. The jug is in two tones, rose-violet on the left and brown-violet on the right. The two violets are separated by a mauve-white line around the object.

The slice of pumpkin is sunflower yellow for the flesh and emerald green for the skin. The latter is also used for a fig at the bottom of the picture. It is outlined and isolated in white. Its plate is iron-gray with a touch of violet, outlined in white or violet-white.

We have, as in *The Sickle*, three independent figurations clearly detached from each other. On one hand there is the round table with brown horizontal lines, on the other the background in three vertical planes which repeats the thick texture and colors from the jug in the *Skull and Jug* (pink in the middle, brown on the edges). The jug is continued at the bottom by a sort of black shadow bordered by gray-brown, the plate by a short shadow and a figuration in slanting brown lines, touched with light yellow spots where it meets the plate.

The space in both works is a non-dimensional, almost level "total space" in which are inscribed the objects which are part of a tactile space. The result of these two spaces is an absolute pictorial space not divisible into elements bound by proximity in a depth of perspective. The objects are projected forward but better and more so than in the Cubist technique. They cannot be disassociated from the whole except by their color value. But if one looks at the picture carefully one sees that they are part of the whole, being reintegrated in their surrounding backgrounds, which are complementary and stabilizing both in form and colors.

These pictures, which might be dark, are on the contrary highly luminous. The light colors certainly count for a good deal in this, but the white contours are the essential element of the luminosity as they are that of the color harmony.

Here again it seems to me there is a meaning which transcends the plastic poetic creation. In *The Sickle* one sees hanging from a nail (which recalls the nail of the Cubist period) a chain which continues on the table as far as the lower edge of the picture; then a stoneware pot and a sickle. In *The Pumpkin* we see a slice of lemon, a pot and barely indicated, a chain. May one not find in these two works an allusion to work in the fields? The sickle and the long chain in that case represent the pitiless labor which chains the peasant to the earth. The pumpkin is the fruit of labor, the chain being here partly effaced. But it is always present. Work must be recommenced and the earth labored, harrowed and sown for there to be a harvest.

Billiards.

"*Billiards*" *(Le Billard)* (1945). By reason of intimate knowledge and long study of it in the Musée d'Art Moderne, we propose to analyze this version of "Billiards" in width (1.50 × 1.94). Another version, which could be seen at the Galerie Maeght before it left for Mexico, increases even further the sensation of verticality and breaking up, and it is that one which we reproduce (Pl. 117). There is a third (1.45 × 1.55) in the Collection of Mr. Leigh Bloch in Chicago.

The presentation of the picture, that of the Musée d'Art Moderne, is extremely curious and even paradoxical. The billiard table is on the right, vertical in a third of its surface, and ascending leftwards in the other two thirds. Placed edgeways, it is almost stuck up against the background walls of the room. The planes of the walls, as in *The Yellow Tablecloth* (Pl. 84) but in a different fashion, balance the aberrant suggestions of the broken-up billiard table by opposing each other in two directed thrusts. The total space results from a rhythmic and figurative construction brought about by the merging of opponent elements.

If we take into account the space of *The Yellow Tablecloth* and the broken-up table in an X construction of the *Three Lemons* or *The Green Tablecloth*, we possess the two essential figurative elements of *Billiards*: the construction of a visual and tactile pictorial space by coordinates, some of which are non-realist (the broken-up tables) and the others (the wall angles) are part of the composition and help to realize the space in multiple directions. This space unites all the possibilities already used but not yet articulated as they are in *Billiards*.

The billiard table is seen edgeways, that is to say resting on one of its sides. The green cloth is thus vertical and on it are three balls in a triangle and two crossed cues. It is not a question, properly speaking, of a tilted billiard table, but of a table whose third dimension, that of depth, has been reduced to the vertical plane. It is a survival of Cubist ideology and in this way it is understandable that the three balls and the cues should be placed on it as if it were not vertical. The breaking-up is another survival of Cubism: the two planes of the table correspond to two vertical planes in juxtaposition.

Behind the billiard table is the top of a round table which is also reduced vertically. It has on it a pot of flowers with long leaves which is in a normal position. Slightly to the left, almost in the center of the canvas, is a radio set and behind it, half a small square table with a thick book on it. The background wall starts with a window with a large diamond-shaped grating. There follows a sort of fluted pilaster, then a small section of wall, then another, making an angle with the former one, and finally a curtained door.

Two spaces are merged: 1) the Cubist space, which is that of the reductions; 2) an almost normal space (the elements of the still life, the window and the walls). The reason for this is to obtain an absolutely vertical composition.

The figuration also is ideologically double: 1) *non-realist*, where it is a question not of the appearance of the billiard table but of its reduction by 90º on to the vertical plane, and of its breaking-up; 2) *realist*, (in so far as Braque ever can be realist). All the objects, and above all the table, are represented much as they are in reality, taking into account the transcription into paint.   The pot is such as Braque paints them, stylized and two-toned like the table on which it is set.

This superposition of two spaces and the double figuration of aspect make us ask once more how it is done.   Is it the construction of a visual space?   Yes, but without depth because of the absolutely vertical composition.   The angle of the wall has the function of establishing a short third dimension which is realized by the small table and book behind the billiard table, the pedestal table with the pot of leaves and the radio set. We have: 1) a first level, that of the billiard table, 2) a second plane, the pedestal table and the radio set, 3) a third plane, the table and book, and 4) the walls.

The tactile space is entirely defined by the three planes which separate us from the objects, and the objects from each other, the latter being situated at imaginable distances.

The total space is the sum of them, and thus becomes a pictorial space but without closing upon itself or going in multiple directions, as it does in the *Femme au Miroir*.

It may be asked why the billiard table is in two zones, one horizontal and the other slanting.   They are equivalent to Cubist implied juxtaposed planes and have perhaps a further plastic significance.

The angle made by the break-up is added to the wall-angle.   The vertical line of the break is the continuation of the line of the wall-angle.   The picture is divided into two parts, that on the right occupying almost a third of the surface, and that on the left the other two-thirds.

We must now return to the balls and billiard cues.   The cues are crossed in a flat X, making two angles, and, more important still, giving two directions.   The upper cue makes a V with the ascending top of the billiard table which it compensates.   The lower cue is parallel in direction to the same edge, which it prolongs where the other compensates it.

The balls suggest a triangle whose base is the virtual line which unites the possible virtual lines from the ascending part to the peak, marked by the one ball in the angle where the cues cross.   This triangle increases the slant of the ascending zone as much as it balances, by opposition, the triangle of cues on the right in the horizontal zone.

To sum up, this arrangement is the structure of the whole lower part of the picture, the billiard table.

To proceed, the ascending part of the billiard table is a mass whose upper angle invades the left of the picture.   To balance it Braque has placed symmetrically on the right, the *round* table, the *round* pot and ts *curved* leaves.   The radio set and the book occupy the middle of the canvas.   They diminish the heavy thrust of the ascending billiard table and center the picture.

The background is like a frame (we recall the *Figures in Composition*).   The curtain and the door on the left correspond to the window and pilaster on the right, and the moldings on the ceiling complete the frame.   The lightness of the window, the pilaster, the plane of the wall and of the still life, balance in their diversity, both of lightness and of the objects themselves, the vast but empty wall on the left.

The picture is thus constructed horizontally in two zones: the first with figuration of objects, at the bottom; the second, without figuration of objects, above.   The whole weight of the work rests on the bottom either vertically or obliquely.

At the end of 1945, which we have now reached, and in 1946, Braque's work continued with variations, using his most recent technical acquisitions as well as his oldest, the latter renewed by different presentation. I invite the reader to find for himself, by careful examination of the pictures reproduced, the components which I have analyzed at some length, so that he may recognize in them the old themes of which they are variations.   I propose for the year 1946 the *Double Still Life with Flowers* (Pl. 123) and *The Sunflowers* (Pl. 116).   In the latter the still life encircled by curves over-runs the painted framing, with the angles or rounded edges of the tablecloth.

But the year 1946 is above all that of *La Femme au Miroir*.

TOTAL SPACE

THE *Femme au Miroir* (1946; Pl. 124) is for me the most complete realization of the pictorial fact in a totally pictorial space, whose poetic plastic form implies a lyric poetic creation. The picture is made up as follows. On the right, the whole height of the canvas is a dressing-table with descending surface, with a basin and a mirror. On the left, three-quarters of the height of the canvas, is a woman seated in front of the dressing-table and mirror. Around the head of the woman and the mirror are curved lines. We recognize figurations we know such as the profile of the woman with a marine background, and curved planes.

The whole picture is an upward thrust, so powerful that it over-runs the top of the canvas, as, by hinting at something different above, it allows the imagination thus provoked to construct a sort of world of cupolas, a world which would open high above on to a night filled with constellations of stars; a world with strange curves, suggesting both an observatory and the bathysphere of undersea explorers. We feel ourselves lost in this space, which has nothing to do with that in which we live ordinarily.

In the *Pink Tablecloth* (1933; Pl. 79) and in *Billiards* (1945; Pl. 117), the first made up of curves and the second of straight lines, the space, though unusual and recreated by the painter to form a poetic representation of a purely plastic order, did not embarrass us; we accepted the work such as it was, as we soon discovered the directive ideas which gave the figurations their forms. The work was a pictorial fact only. In *La Femme au Miroir* this is no longer the case.

The pictorial fact is not immediately evident. We feel that it exists and that it is preponderant, but that we will only discover it later, when we are trying to understand the why and how of this dazzling work, and by what extraordinary plastic means we have been so disturbed, mind and soul lost and absorbed by reason of the fact that whichever way we turn our glance, we are first confused and then enclosed in a sort of gravitation of spheres, or rather, spherical construction, which seem to be added to each other without any possible end.

Look at the woman in front of the mirror. Her profile is that of the *Woman with Marine Background*. Why? Should we look for something other than a plastic theme? Have they not the same female nature? In front of her mirror and dressing-table where she is going to perfect her face by artificial means, is she not the mysterious creature, the original Eve, as dangerous as the siren from the sea? We can now understand better the extraordinary atmosphere which surrounds her. The siren was plunged in a deadly sea in which

one cannot breathe; the woman at the mirror is surrounded by a wandering world which imprisons us, without any possible end except further dizziness !

If we look again we see that a thin, a very thin line divides the work in two vertically, exactly between the dressing-table mirror and the female figure, and we may ask what this line signifies, and if it has any other but plastic importance. It exists in the *Woman with Mandolin* of 1937 (Pl. 89) and also in the *Figures in Composition*. It serves to separate two colored planes, one darker and one lighter. We will find it again in other pictures, dividing the canvas into two figurations. In this *Femme au Miroir* we could suppress it (in thought) without harming the balance of the composition, which is in dominant browns. One can therefore attribute to it another role, that of separating the woman from her mirror, not figuratively but poetically, the original Eve from the appearance she wishes to have.

And finally, if we divide the picture arbitrarily in two by an imaginary horizontal line going from the woman's shoulder to the bottom of the mirror, a line which would also be the horizontal median, we see that everything which is painted below it is of an extraordinary figurative complexity, whereas everything above it is painted in large planes.

66

What can we conclude from this? The bottom of the picture is strictly and materially human; the top is its spiritual rival. It is the same as in the *Woman with Marine Background* (Pl. 104) in which the sexual bust offered its human feminine reality, while the double visage summoned up dark and unreal ecstasy.

Does this extraordinary space which surrounds the woman at her dressing-table signify her isolation? Like every other woman in front of a mirror she is a prisoner at the same time of her person, her personality and her character: what she is physically, what she is psychologically and what she would like to be. This space was perhaps conceived and realized by Braque because the theme of Feminity suggested it to him not only plastically but even more, poetically.

It is no longer the patch of white which becomes the tablecloth, nor the lemon and orange which become fruit, it is Eve imprisoned by the Temptation. If man is her prisoner, she is also her own prisoner. The Tree of Knowledge and the cunning Serpent have revealed to her but one thing, her power and her subjection. The *Eve Tempted* in the Autun Museum by an unknown sculptor of genius of the 12th century, shows her, with most perturbing face, plunged in the giddy discoveries of revelation. Braque will have her no longer tempted but a temptress, encircled by Fate.

Taking a last look at the picture we see that the bottom is of an extremely complicated figuration, while the top is constructed entirely by curved planes. Behind the chair, at the bottom on the right, is sketched a wall with plinths, and immediately above it another wall drawn in the shape of a cross but which cannot be on the same plane. This wall is visible through an opening in the shape of an ellipse made in a sort of revolving cabin, and it has a curve like the interior of a sphere, which one finds prolonged at the top of the canvas. The whole picture ascends toward the open ceiling. The only straight lines are to be found in the lower half; principally vertical, with a few horizontal and slanted ones (the back of the chair, the woman's arm, the dressing-table, the basin and the wall with plinths); the others are curved, going in almost every direction, but always ascending and increasing.

Where do we find a visual space and a tactile space? — Visual space. The successive spheres are certainly separated from each other and in consequence seem farther and farther away from us, I mean farther away from us and the central group of the woman and dressing-table. But this visual space is stifling, unorthodox, abnormal, belonging to a world of fiction. It is a pure creation of the mind translated plastically and into paint. — Tactile space. We are in effect separated from the dressing-table, the mirror and the seated woman, a group which is entirely bound together by the merging of the lines which draw it, and this group is distinct from the curved walls which surround it. We can touch the woman, the chair, the dressing-table and the mirror... even the wall with plinths. But after that, what we touch is not an end but a temporary limitation... the walls of a labyrinth.

What is astonishing in the picture is this. If we look at the bottom only, it is normal, a matter of a table with a basin on it, a chair on which a woman is seated and a wall with plinths and framing. When we reach the woman's face everything becomes abnormal. The mirror is made up of curved lines, the woman's head is a replica (in profile) of that of the *Woman with a Marine Background* and we are lost in the universe of a spherical labyrinth. The woman who up till then was a woman preparing to make up her face in order to please, becomes an almost arbitrary image; she signifies a fatality from which neither she herself nor those to whom she will offer her face can escape, but are shut up at once in a prison without exit.

"I want an object to lose its usual function," writes Braque and adds: "it is only art which can give it a universal character..."

"What was at first a patch of white becomes a tablecloth, a plastic creation becomes a poetic one..."

"A painting which does not disturb you, what is it worth?"

THE STUDIO SERIES AND THE BIRDS

BRAQUE seems to have had several different preoccupations in his last eight years of painting. Not that he has changed; M. Jean Cassou is absolutely right when he says: "Every picture by Braque marks an acquisition since the preceding one; one cannot find in his progress any break in the continuity or any contradiction... Braque, or Constancy Rewarded..."

Braque adds to himself incessantly. What he acquires is the complement of what he has already acquired; what he innovates is a new aspect of something which already exists in his work.

The years 1947-1955 bring both a purification and a plus-value. The purification leads almost to asceticism; the plus-value is the comprehensive vision of what a picture can be, according to his conception of it. The purification has resulted in work such as *The Chair* (Pl. 126; 1947), *The Packing Case* (Pl. 125; 1948) and the *Double Still Life with Flowers* (Pl. 123; 1948), and the comprehensive vision in the *Studios* (1948-49 to 1955), a few large allegorical figures such as *Night* (Pl. 136; 1951) and some very small gray seascapes, almost monochrome, which give a very anti-Boudin and anti-Impressionist idea of the Channel at Dieppe, as what they represent is not the sea and sky, fertile in prodigious coloring, but everything in them which is disturbing and disquieting.

Whatever the pictures may be, it is always the problem of the representation of space which dominates them. At the beginning of 1955 Braque said to Mr. John Richardson: "All my life my great preoccupation has been to paint space." But in these canvases space is no longer the essential aim, it is only a constituent element.

The asceticism appears in two ways. The first might be called an asceticism of line and texture of which *The Chair* is very representative. The second is an asceticism of subject and the pictures which show it best are *The Packing Case*, and the *Double Still Life with Flowers* in 1948, and *Night* in 1951.

In *The Chair* there is no more than an iron garden-chair with two pieces of fruit on the seat. Everything is in curved or angular lines; there is hardly any material except vigorous impasto in the upper right-hand part of the background.

The wooden *Packing Case* is stamped with the letters BAS HAUT and has a pot of flowers on it; there is nothing else. Its simplicity is as moving as a Van Gogh, like *The Chair* which is exactly *his chair*.

68

In the *Double Still Life with Flowers* (Pl. 123) the picture is divided in two by a vertical line. This median is that of the *Femme à la Toilette* and the other pictures mentioned in the preceding chapter. On the right we have one picture and on the left another, which oppose each other even though they have points in common. The left hand picture consists of a glass pot on a round table of dark coloring, and these occupy the lower half. The upper half is separated into strips by long branches with leaves and flowers on a mural décor. That on the right has a triangular table with vertical legs on which is set a stoneware vase filled with large leaves. Pot, table and leaves have the same over-all light tint. The forms of the objects are demarcated by a white line. The dark background recalls the table in the left hand picture.

Night is a very tall gray figure on a black background; an immobile face with horned brow, almost the face of a witch or an oracular Pythoness.

The Studios are spaced out from 1939 up to the present day. In 1939 Braque had already painted two of a rare beauty (Pl. 90 and 95). One, *The Painter and his Model*, stands out among the *Figures in Composition*; the other, as we have noticed, was of extreme figurative complexity and it is this complexity, though in a different form, that we shall find again.

Braque was inspired in this series of pictures both by his Paris studio and that of Varengeville. One finds, though not in all of them, the theme of the *Bird*, whether sitting or in flight, the bird which he had already painted in 1948 on a canvas subsequently destroyed, and which is also the theme of the Louvre Museum ceiling (1952-1953). There is a spatial image in it, the bird, a spatial being *par excellence*, who traverses space in all directions in the course of his flight.

Although they differ, the *Studios* can be grouped according to two principal themes. The first, relatively simple, is a constant and Nos. I and IV retain the form of the *Studios and Interiors* as the painter had already often conceived them.

The four others on the other hand are truly for Braque "the studio seen as a mirage," as Mr. John Richardson observes in the remarkable studies he has devoted to them (Burlington Magazine, June 1955 and L'Œil 1955). It is in these that the theme of the bird appears.

In *Studio II*, (Pl. 128) the composition is highly complex. The whole picture, woven vertically both by lines and by the form of the objects, attains an extraordinary density. The multiple objects or figurations which constitute it are juxtaposed, either side by side or one behind the other. It is pure tactile space. One would say that Braque wished to paint all the conceivable themes of a still life in such a way that one could touch them in imagination, so close are they to us and to each other. The upper part is dominated by an immense stylized bird on the right. At the bottom, in the opposite direction to the bird, is an enormous light arrow.

In *Studio III*, (Pl. 129) there is less complication. It is also "woven" vertically. On the left is an easel in the shape of a cross with a small painting on it. In the center, at the bottom, are a palette and three brushes and then a circular decoration of Mozarabic type, in ochre and green. Above, still on the right, is the stylized bird in flight.

Studio V, which we reproduce (Pl. 130), is perhaps one of the most luxuriant of Braque's works and is indescribable. Once again we have the bird flying across from right to left.

A *Studio VII* (1949-1955) is still unfinished in the artist's studio. In it we find the palette, the large jar, an arrow at the bottom left, much smaller than in *Studio II*, and also the bird flying above from right to left.

In *Studio II*, and *Studio VI*, we may notice also the left female profile similar to that in the *Still Life* of 1938 (Pl. 85) and in several sculptures.

All these works are notable for their dark tints, the initial preparation of the canvas being an almost black foundation. The last, however, *Studio VIII* (1954-1955) in the Douglas Cooper collection (Pl. 132) is of a richness of color exceptional in Braque's work. It is a triumph of red, green and blue, with the great white splash of the bird above, balanced toward the bottom by two white triangles which recall the arrow in *Studio II*. One feels in this luminous canvas that the artist has solved the conflict of space and color, which made him say paradoxically to Dora Vallier (*Cahiers d'Art* 1955): "I felt that color might give sensations which could trouble space and that is why I abandoned it".

It is remarkable that the *Studio* series, although spectacularly new, is profoundly related to everything that Braque has painted. One can find in it numerous elements of earlier works, used in a different way.

But that, I think, is not the essential. The question is whether this series, with its concentration of themes and objects will lead Braque to revise, with a view to enrichment, the pictorial space as we have tried to analyze and define it; the space which has never seemed to him impossible of attainment, but whose last form is never the final and definitive one.

In 1952 Braque was commissioned to paint a ceiling in three panels for a room in the Louvre Museum. When M. Georges Salles, Director of National Museums, decided to renovate the decoration of the ceilings in the Louvre, confronting modern masters with the celebrated Delacroix ceiling in the Apollo Gallery, it seemed a bold step to take, but it was rapidly justified. Braque's ceiling, great black birds ringed with white in a deep blue sky with white patches, dominates with its ritual flight the celebrated Louvre Tomb, the most important reminder of Etruscan civilization (Pl. 133).

In the same line of studies there was a moving *Dead Bird at the Foot of the Ladder* which the artist saw fit to destroy, and there is also one of his favorite canvases *The Bird and its Nest* (1955; Pl. p. 13). The bird in full flight, still in his studio, which he calls *On the Wing* (Pl. 134), with the great splash of black recalling the past night, in which a crescent moon can be distinguished, and with its light blue background, and thick patches of white lead impasto which catch the light, continues and completes with an even greater poetic simplicity the great birds of the Louvre.

The repeated appearance of the bird theme at the peak of the Master's career cannot but recall the great cry of Leonardo da Vinci in the evening of his life, quoted by Paul Valéry: "Blasting his imperfectl abor, illuminating his patience and the obstacles he encountered by the apparition of a supreme spiritual life, an obstinate certitude: the great bird will take its first flight mounted on a great swan; filling the universe with wonder and all that is written with its glory, and eternal praise to the nest in which it was born."

DRAWINGS, ENGRAVINGS AND SCULPTURES

BRAQUE has drawn comparatively little, if by "drawing" we mean everything in his work which is not painted, that is to say, drawings (in the proper sense), dry points, etchings, lithographs and "engraved plasters." But if he has drawn but little, (quite apart from the sketches in the drawing books), he has always drawn. In each period and in each phase of his work, the drawings have the appearance and the aesthetic quality particular to the period.

There are drawings or Cubist engravings (Pl. 31) in which one finds the order and the figurative economy of Cubism. Some pictures, the figures in composition, have been either preceded or followed by drawings in which the picture appears in a fragmentary state. At the time of the *Canephorae* Braque drew some admirable *Nudes* (Pl. 42 and 43) either in crayon, sanguine or pastel. They are sometimes seated, doing their hair, or in a dream-like monumental immobility, and sometimes recumbent, displaying their sensual curves. In 1931 for the beach pictures, and in 1934 for the *Still Lifes* with encircling curves, we have several drawings which either represent them or are variations of them, in black or in sanguine. The double visage of the *Woman with Marine Background* which is also that of the *Femme au Miroir* was drawn and then engraved, to become "Sao."

The engraved plasters are creations of Braque's; on a layer of plaster is placed a coating of black, and on the black the painter incises what he wants to represent. He may also remove large slices of the black coating so that the white reappears, and can be colored if necessary. This so-called "engraved" plaster is thus properly speaking a drawing.

It is to be remarked that the engraved figures on plaster are taken from mythology: *Sao, Herakles, Io,* etc. and are delineated with extreme suppleness. The curves which cross, overlap and continue again, confer, in their sinuous relationship, an almost aerial and highly transparent appearance on the characters. That of *Sao* is to be found in several engraved plasters and in many drawings.

When Braque pursues a theme, he seeks its linear elements by every sort of process. It may be a lithograph, colored after, as in *Helios*, or it may start with a dry point and end up by stages in a lithograph, of which a remarkable example is the *Teapot with Lemon*. He may even prepare the way for a lithograph study with an oil painting, as in the *Athena* of 1932. In the same year an engraved plaster *Herakles* is anticipated by an etching *Goddess on Horseback*.

I think that what interests Braque most, perhaps because it is both a drawing and a beginning of a picture, is color lithography. He knows all the subtleties of its technique. The same subject, first treated in black, with numerous variants in the black valves, can end up in color. The *Teapot with Lemon* is one of the most successful of these.

He likes lithographs to be "framed," that is to say inscribed in an oblong quadrilateral with round corners, which reminds one of a cinema screen. It is the case with the teapot (above), with engraved plasters and with a lithograph of wonderful movement, *Io.*

This latter, like the engraved plasters with mythological themes, may lead us to ask why mythology took up so large a place in Braque's mind. I think we must look for an answer in the beginnings of his career. He certainly, like all painters, frequented the Louvre, but he never had a desire to be impregnated by its pictures. His admiration for the Masters which he contemplated conduced to deference but not to imitation. If truth be told, he frequented the Sculpture Rooms more than the Painting Rooms, and among the former, particularly those of pre-Classical Greek art. He drew no lessons from them, nor the prototype of forms; only themes which were later to becomes *Helios, Io, Sao, Herakles,* myths, in fact, which are quite the contrary of anecdote as they symbolize ideas. He became impregnated with these ideas; he wished to be obsessed by them to the point of hallucination and he has represented them as he felt them, and as he saw them in his mind's eye.

The drawings and engraved plasters give us two aspects of Braque's "graphism": sometimes as in *Phix* (Pl. p. 76) wit is very direct, conceived with almost typographical simplicity, while at the same time evoking archaic Greek or Egyptian styles; at others it is a subtle intertwining of curved lines, the kind of drawing which characterizes most of the plates in the *Theogony* and a good number of plasters.

Engraved plasters, engravings and mythological drawings tended to develop figuratively around a central literary idea, to a plastic transcription of a written story, and, if I may be allowed to say it, to an abstraction even more abstract. Braque has also given us the admirable etchings which illustrate *The Theogony of Hesiod* (1955; begun in 1932).

Can one speak of illustrations in the ordinary sense of the word? In the course of twenty years of preparation he became impregnated (his favorite word) by his subject. We can count several hundred drawings in the Drawing Books which relate to it and practically all the engraved plasters were conceived as studies for the great final realization.

As there are comparatively few drawings in Braque's work, so are there but few sculptures, and those of small dimensions. He is profoundly a painter, by temperament as well as by profession; he thinks and feels in color. Sculpture must at some point or other embarrass him; first because it does not admit or barely admits color, secondly because it is necessarily three-dimensional, and finally because it can transcribe nothing beyond what is anecdotal. All this is contrary to Braque's aesthetic system and to his sensibility. But what may have tempted him was the "plastic" side of sculpture, possibly as a material and even total realization of tactile space, that is to say touching an object no longer in imagination but in reality.

In 1922 he modeled a statuette, a Nude, which associates in schematic form, or rather in an evolving of curves from top to bottom, the round contours of the female body. This silhouette in "contours" did not seem to him to admit of sexual attributes and he replaced them by geometrical figurations. He later made other copies of this nude.

He also sculpts birds, including an *Ibis* (1945), the form of which some have thought to find in the last *Studios*, though we may be permitted to wonder why. But above all he sculpted wonderful *Ponies*, both in 1939 and in 1946. In this latter work he kept only the head, whose admirably proportioned lines suffice to give the impression of a gallop.

In the first year of the war, 1939, while living at Varengeville, Braque for a while made use of the shingle on the beach. These sculptures have been called "sculptures on shingle," but the word is deceptive. The stone is that of the North Sea cliffs, which is chalk. From the soft stones of the strand Braque constructed profiles (Pl. p. 74) or combinations of forms (Pl. p. 74), also in profile.

In 1942 he sculpted an extremely curious *Fish.* Its body and head are a simple edged diamond, starting from which a horizontal line ends in the tail. Divided into four, the body has stripes in different directions and the indication of an eye: a triangular fin hangs under the belly. It seems as if Cubist composition by planes had some little part in the elaboration of the sculpture.

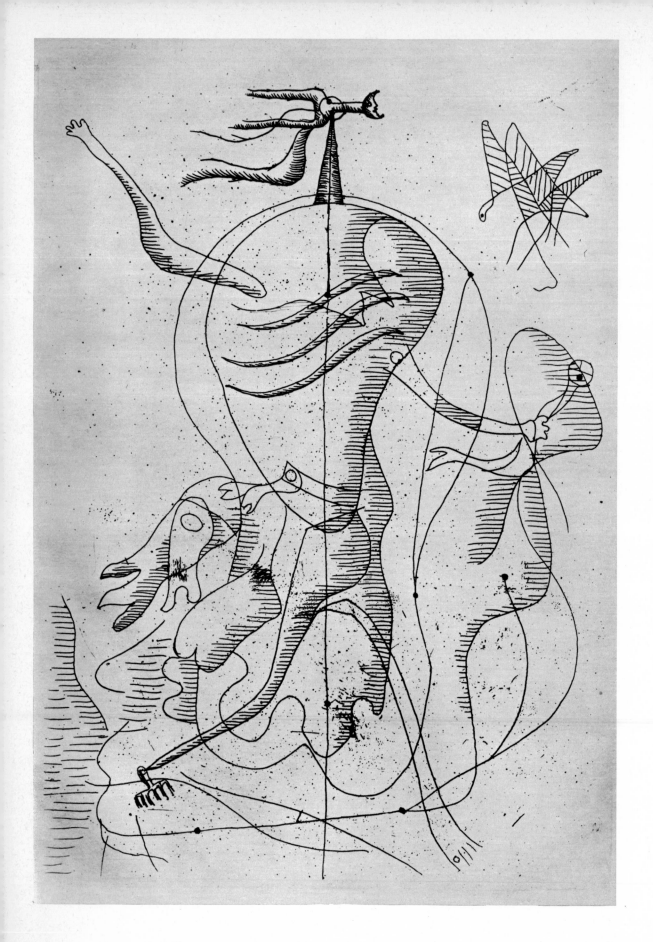

1955
XII PLANCHE DE LA THÉOGONIE
Eau-forte

If there are engraved plasters which may be assimilated to drawings, there are others also in relief. On a black foundation, Braque disposes lines or masses in relief. The masses are as if in impasto; they most often reproduce the mythological themes already used. In 1935 it is *Io*, and this *Io*, in plaster in relief, is the prefiguration of the color lithography of 1945. It is repeated in inverted form in *The Chariot* of 1952 (Pl. 122).

We might say that these drawings, engravings and lithographs were done by Braque by way of diversion or perhaps more as "interludes" in the sense given to the word by Giraudoux in his "Intermezzo." They are a period of fruitful repose in the middle of work, a time of meditation between two "phases." Their value is not lessened by this; it is of another order, indeed of a quite different nature from that of the painted pictures in which his whole personality is in play. Though they be no more than particular technical problems, a sort of craftman's amusement, let us repeat once more that the craftsmanship in Braque's work must never be underestimated. Without it, Braque would not be what he is: a master in both senses of the word, as one speaks of a master cabinet-maker, or a master glass-blower, a title which implies a new creative action by means of art.

While for Matisse or Dufy, drawing is practically remaking a picture without its colors, and for Picasso it is an act of manual virtuosity, for Braque it is an act of virtuosity as spiritual as it is manual. What has been done, or what will be done in paint, seems to find a kind of compromise, a half-way stage, in drawing, in engraving and even more in lithography.

Lithography, especially in color, is a constructive as well as a representative material, the importance of which for Braque is almost as great as the poetic creation, in which it is an element since it creates the "level of appearance." We should not be astonished therefore by the minute care and attention which he gives to its execution. Nothing escapes him since everything is predetermined.

I doubt whether Braque's drawings occupy the place they deserve. They are not well known and it is true that they are rare. A few privileged people have been allowed to go through the portfolios in the master's studio, and a few recent books allow one to form an idea of the work. If the general public knew it, they would be astonished. For it is not simply an accompaniment to a painting, as it is for Matisse, a sketch for a picture, in fact its figurative evolution, as it is for Dufy, or a different aesthetic or lyrical state, as it is for Picasso. It is a different poetic creation, in a pure state, without the prestige and attraction of color.

CONCLUSION

GEORGES BRAQUE'S place in th history of Art can never be sufficiently emphasized. Even if his work were not what it is artistically, I mean less admirable and of lesser genius, he would still remain a creator of forms as well as the instigator and initiator of an aesthetic system: Cubism.

It was in reference to his work that Louis Vauxcelles in 1907 spoke of cubes and cubism. It was Braque who first adopted musical instruments as themes and pretexts for painting, and he who introduced lettering and " papiers collés " into pictures. He was the first to paint with a sand foundation, on plaster, and on masses of white lead and it was he who conceived engraved plasters. He invented the extraordinary and so often disturbing double visages and finally he, and he alone, discovered a pictorial space which owes nothing to anybody.

Certainly one cannot confuse a painting by Matisse with one by Dufy, but even if one hesitates about the attribution of a picture to Braque or Picasso in their period of Analytical Cubism, it is impossible not to be profoundly struck by any work of the former. They have neither the fantasy of Dufy nor the extraordinary equilibrium of Matisse nor yet the agressive arrogance of Picasso but they have a " charm " in the etymological sense of the word which is a " spell " to which one submits, in fact, by impregnation, obsession and hallucination.

Claude Debussy, at the end of his life, wanted to add to his name the designation particularly dear to him, of " French Composer. " He had the right to it. Braque does not ask for it but one might bestow it on him without any scruple.

I know well that Matisse and Dufy are also profoundly French, though in a different manner. Matisse is a Cartesian who, following Delacroix and Renoir but expurgating from the first his anecdotal romanticism and from the second his carnal sensuality, aims at the " clear and distinct " precision fathered by the author of the *Discours sur la Méthode*. This " accounting of values " (the words are Dufy's) is peculiar to France. What do Racine and Molière give us? (I will not include Boileau as he is most often a mere accountant of commonplaces.) A balanced distribution of tragic and comic emotions, allowing in each case the least amount of provocation sufficient for the maximum effect.

78

Dufy has inherited from the 18 th century its effortless grace (in appearance only!) and the charming fantasy which mask, too often, the power and the careful precision of his work.

Braque is anti-Cartesian. He makes use of controlled intuition and he knows what he wants. Every work of his is an "approximation," as Charles du Bos would have said, or what Mallarmé would have called an " experiment with a view to improvement. " His " poetic creation " is the contrary of romanticism, which does not appear in his work. The man and the painter make one person and the painter always dominates the man. Making a picture is not a question of exaltation for him; he is content with fervor.

It is in this that he is profoundly French and is the great line of the Classical Masters. For his classicism is the contrary of academicism. He renews himself incessantly by beginning again, not in another guise but by being more himself than ever. I said that he knows what he wants, but we may ask whether, every time he paints a picture, he knows how he wants it. For he wants it to be both representative and constructive of a certain poetical and spatial condition; he wants it always to be essential, and to culminate in a pictorial whole of flawless craftsmanship, visual attraction and structure, from which should radiate a poetic super-reality, a lyricism not overpowering but haunting. It is impregnation, obsession and hallucination which, when his contemplation is over, should make the spectator feel the sacerdotal value of the picture, the exhaustive greatness of its art.

For Matisse, painting is a chromatic problem to be solved; for Dufy it is the insertion of an anecdote, more or less fragile, in a " pictorial fact, " while for Picasso it is a matter of giving vent to a suppressed emotion or some form of aggressive anarchism. For Braque it is a question of transcending everyday reality and raising it to an aesthetic value.

Perhaps the most striking aspect of his work is its continuity. True, he has passed through a Fauve period and a Cubist period and returned from time to time to a sort of reality; but he has always maintained the same discipline.

The Fauve paintings by Braque are disciplined, as we have tried to show. As for Cubism, it professes the strictest of disciplines and Braque himself was the creator and instigator of this novel and constructive doctrine. He never departed from it. Even when he no longer painted in the Cubist manner, its discipline remained valid for him, since it has no other aim but to give the rules and the means to achieve a painting which should be no more than a pictorial fact constructed according to a pictorial space. If Cubism was first considered revolutionary, anarchical and formless, it revealed itself, when the period of trial and experiment was over, as the logic of the thought and plastic representation which resulted from it. It expressed exactly Braque's thought, his aesthetic system and his technique.

This discipline, both of spirit and of craftsmanship, which makes him a painter and nothing but a painter, can probably be traced to his youth when he was learning and working at the decoration of apartments. For him painting consists of manipulating painting material and representing forms which, when he passed from craftsmanship to art, became poetic. The orange and the lemon became fruit.

Matisse achieves this also, but not in its essential poetic meaning. For him the orange and the lemon are always an orange and a lemon, supporting a color by a form. The orange is an absolute orange and the lemon an absolute lemon, and moreover they are fruits chosen for their plastic value.

From all this it results that Braque's place in the continuity of French painting is that of a Master. When Blaise Cendrars writes of him: " Every picture by Braque is a lecture, a panegyric and a prayer, " he speaks the truth. It is a lecture by reason of its masterly teaching, and a panegyric in its power and greatness. The prayer is the fervor of the artist communicating with his art.

André Salmon wrote in " *Art Vivant*": " Georges Braque has acquired the right to be called the leader of a school. " This is exact, since he was the creator of Cubism, lettering and *papiers collés*, and also the originator of " poetic creation " and even more of pictorial space. If many young painters are still haunted and bewildered by the work of Picasso, and others dazzled by the juxtaposed colors of Matisse, when they feel themselves being swallowed up, why do they not meditate on the lesson of Braque: that true, original personality is the result of long patience and perpetual meditation and that it is only acquired by progressive stages of enrichment.

This continuity, this constancy, this perpetual sacrifice has been called by Braque " spirituality, " as opposed to ideality. It is the poetic creation, the enriching meaning; but it is also, and perhaps more than anything, classicism. Classical works, such as we find in French 17 th century literature, transcend the accidental, the fortuitous and the actual, to aim at what is essential, durable and outside time. For a classical writer, as for Braque, the orange and the lemon are no more than fruit, fervor is sufficient, since exaltation is superabundant. The lesson of Braque is a true lesson in classicism as it shows that what is sufficient only is necessary. His works are neither disturbing hor exalting, they ask only for contemplation and meditation, proceeding, from what is "spectacularly" represented to what is "poetically" induced. One "sees" a picture, one "feels" it, one "understands" it, and finally one "submits" to it. Impregnation, Obsession, Hallucination.

Braque is not a revolutionary painter. He has said so and added "fervor is enough for me". He has also written: "I am for the rule which corrects the emotion"; "Limited means engender new forms, invite creation and make style..."; "Progress in art does not consist of extending its limits but of getting to know them better." These last two statements sum up Braque's art admirably. He knows what he wants, pictorial space, and the means to attain it. These means are for him the most interesting part of the work as they alone allow him reach his goal. "I do not do what I want, I do what I can."

It is understandable that for some people a picture by Braque is a calculated, predetermined work, in its perfection, in the fact that nothing can be taken from it or added to it without destroying its perfect balance. This is a tribute to the painter's genius, but it is also an error. "I do not do what I want, I do what I can." And yet he says also: "The picture is finished when the painter has effaced the idea. The idea is what "ties up" the picture." It is here that the painter's personality comes into play. He has the idea of the picture, a schematic theme. He must make the picture, and bit by bit in the course of making it, he creates it, partially and successively. But he is also influenced by what he has painted, which dictates to him a certain direction already taken, a certain construction already begun, and relations to be added to those already found. The painter must call on all his intuition, on all the images that rise before his eyes, with the forms appropriate to what he wants from them, in order that his hand may bring them to life from the palette on to the canvas.

Paul Valéry once said that only the first line of a poem is the gift of the gods, those that follow are but rhetoric. I suppose and indeed I believe that it is a question not so much of the first line of a poem, but of the first line found by the poet each time he goes back to work on the same poem. In other words, inspiration is the gift of circumstance. This is probably true also for Braque.

The lyrical condition at the start engenders forms, little by little and by dint of craftsmanship. When the lyrical condition and the forms it induces are exhausted, one must wait for a further lyrical condition and the offspring of that. "I do not do what I want, I do what I can."

Every painter has themes or forms of representation which he prefers and which, if they do not define it, do in some way authenticate the work. Braque naturally has his own.

An English critic who has written one of the best recent studies of Braque's work, Mr. John Richardson, very rightly says that he is "an artist who works habitually in series," by which he means that he can paint a certain number of pictures with an identical subject over a number of years. Mr. Richardson cites the series of *Guéridons*, of beach scenes, of classical figures, of studios. It is true enough and we may ask why Braque paints in series.

Let us first try to put a little order in the chronology of the "series". I will pass over the Fauve period and also the Cubist period with its notable series of *figures with guitar*. As for the other musical instruments, Braque included them in his pictures because they were to his hand, and because, he says, "their plastic nature and their volume brought them into the realm of still life, as I understood it." I was already on the road to tactile space, (it was therefore after 1907-1908), or manual space, as I prefer to define it, and the musical instrument, as an object, had the particularity that one could animate it by touching it, and also since, as he repeats in his interview with Mr. Richardson; "All my life my great preoccupation has been to paint space."

What is constant in Braque's work is his essential attachment to stille life, which we note throughout. In French painting only Chardin continued in this genre so steadily. Like Chardin also, Braque cares little for portraying the female face, a few of around 1927, which we know only by photographs, have even been destroyed by him.

An important series, which continued from 1922-1929, is that of the *guéridons* or tables. The choice of this article of furniture seems to me to have lain in its possibility of enlarging Cubist still life. This remained the principle motif of the picture but not the only one. It was added to, both above and below. Then

the tables (with four legs) and the *guéridons* became in their turn motifs in the picture.   The tables allowed the painter to construct a new space, as we have seen, their lateral edges which should have converged in depth, on the contrary diverged.   The *guéridons* contributed important figurations with their round top and highly curved pedestal, from which Braque drew some extraordinary compositions.

The tables and *guéridons*, abandoned and then taken up again, appeared in a new form (*The Yellow Tablecloth, The Pink Tablecloth, Tables with Green Slip*, etc...).   But their repetition in the same period was not caused by lack of imagination; for what should we say in that case of Cézanne, of Monet's *Cathedrals*, Matisse's *Odalisques*, or Dufy's *Regattas*?   It was in the very nature of his experiments.   When finished, a picture with the theme of a *guéridon* or a table, did not leave Braque entirely satisfied; the picture might satisfy him as such, but the chosen theme was not exhausted.

The period of the *guéridons* is also that of the *chimney*-pieces, the *billiard tables* and the *green tables*, but in these latter two, there is a new experiment, inaugurated by *The Three Lemons* (1942; Pl. 98), with the structure or rather the breaking-up, in the form of an X, which allows a particular equilibrium in space. Each of the "Billiards" series is different; they all repeat the theme of the break-up, but in each case Braque produces different results from it.

For Mr. Richardson, the "classical figures" are those of the *Canephorae* of 1923-1926.   Though they resemble each other anatomically, their attitudes vary.   Each picture is for Braque a problem to be solved, in which is included an idea, and this idea which varies must be worked on again in a number of figures and in different pictures.   It is not because it is easy or because of lack of imagination that he returns to it, on the contrary it is from scrupulousness, from the need for a totality, from an excessive imagination which one, two or even three pictures cannot satisfy.

He finds in this a gymnastic exercise both for the intellect and for the act of painting and a virtuosity in the creation of different or renewed relations.   It reminds one of those great chess players who play a number of different games simultaneously.

As for the *Beach Scenes* of 1932, we have analyzed them sufficiently for it to be grasped that each version is more than a variation, it is an enrichment; and we may add that there exists in the artist's studio a large *Recumbent* Figure on which he worked from 1932 till 1952.

The theme of the *Studios* provided Braque with several series, in some of which it is treated as an interior with still life (*The Studio* Pl. 95, the *Interior with Palette and Vase of Flowers*, Pl. 110 or that of 1938, Pl. 114 which is remarkable for its large female profile).

From 1937 to 1939 Braque animated his *Studios* with female faces, and we have the series of the *Woman at an Easel*, the *Woman Painter* and the *Painter and his Model* (Pl. 89-93), to which may be related *Patience* of 1942 and even *La Femme au Miroir* of 1946.

The most recent series to date is that of the *Studios* (1949-1955) of which we have already spoken at some length. This series joins up with that of the *Birds*, who took flight from the *Studios* to become independent, as in the pictures *On the Wing* (1955: Pl. 134), and *Bird and its Nest* (Pl. p. 13), and the ceiling of the Salle Henri II in the Louvre.

Thus the repetition of the same objects in his pictures is seen to be no more than a constantly renewed preoccupation with formal research for the "pictorial fact" and "pictorial space."

If the poetic creation in Braque's pictures is such that one can transcend it to find (or to add subjectively) a sense or a meaning of one kind or another, and I have done so in the *Double Figure with Marine Background, Patience, La Femme au Miroir, Vanitas* (in its various versions), *The Sickle* and *The Pumpkin*, if such meanings can be given to a few exceptional pictures, one must not deduce from this that they exist in all of them.

"There have never been any symbols in my painting." The choice of a theme or a subject of figuration is occasioned originally by plastic considerations only. This does not prevent the fact that certain pictures (the *Double Figure* etc...) have acquired in the course of their execution new values from the lyrical contribution proceeding from the lyrical condition which reveals not only formal relations but also relations of poetic significance. It is the same as in certain musical compositions, in which the form is swollen by an emotion which transcends the formal to attain the feelings or the intellect.

May I insist on one point; these added meanings are never anecdotal. Abstract as they are they never leave the realm of *spirituality*. What do we finally apprehend in the *Double Figure with Marine Background*? The double aspect of the woman: her sexual aspect, the "promise of happiness" as Stendhal would say, and the other, almost metaphysical one of the siren, whose charms spell death!

In *Patience*, painted during the Occupation, we are haunted by an atmosphere of anxiety. In *The Pumpkin* and *The Sickle*, it is the "idea" of labor which seems to be evoked; not the labor of a particular peasant: plowing, harrowing, etc... but the profound meaning of the work: laboring continually for a harvest... the cosmic rhythm of which man is an element. This is not anecdote, it is a "spiritual theme."

There is nothing original in his *Vanitas* or his *Skull and Jug*; look at Cézanne and so many others before him. They are what we might almost call a traditional expression of the problem of existence.

It is always a very delicate matter to sound out an artist's purposes in his relations with the eternal, that is to say to discover the religious significance of his work. The fact that Braque painted his various versions of "Vanitas", that he gave a tabernacle door to the church at Assy, or windows to the chapel at Varengeville, does not put an end to the question. But the constant dignity of Braque's work, justifies in the eyes of a Catholic critic, an observation of considerable moral import, which Mr. Michel Florisoone illustrates by a reproduction of the *Bundle of Straw*, a variant of *The Sickle* (Pl. 120): "In art, what is holy is not an added quality, as it can be for certain chosen men; it is the discovery of a profound virtue, existing from the very beginning."

We find ourselves now in the presence of a man and his work, and we have reached the point where this man and his work must impose themselves on us such as they are. Not "*tel qu'en lui-même enfin l'éternité le change*" as with Mallarmé's Edgard Poe, since Braque is still at work in our midst from day to day, but such as he is in himself.

At the beginning of the book we said of Braque that his painting, or better still, art, was for him a priestly task and we may well return now at the end to the exhaustive theme of spirituality. Are not priesthood and spirituality profoundly connected?

For all those who know him, or who have done no more than approach him, Georges Braque, the man, "attracts" by his confusing simplicity, his amiability, and his effacement of himself before his work.

Braque the painter like a sea current, untroubled by storms, winds or tides, pursues his course undeflected by the crazes or fashions of the moment. In his spirituality, he is attracted only by the plastic and poetic value of a "pictorial fact" and is never tempted by an anecdote to be narrated, nor by sensuality, like Matisse, nor by Dufy's joyful vision of life as a spectacle, nor by Picasso's multiple expressions of temperament. It is by reason of this that he is truly a Master.

From Matisse there is nothing to be got but audacities of coloring. Dufy can communicate only his gift for subtle fantasy. And Picasso? Nothing. One cannot repeat Picasso; one can only plagiarise him. But from Braque, everything is to be learnt.

First of all there is the value of craftsmanship in the profession of painter, and then of technique. There follows the value of the *idea* which must preside over, prepare and subordinate the picture to be made and the picture in course of being made. Finally there is the poetic creation which is the spirituality in the work.

But above all one learns from him that the personality of an artist does not consist in a perpetual rivalry and extravagance, but in reflection, and meditation, followed by impregnation, obsession and hallucination, which are slowly translated into the work.

Here are a few of his own aphorisms, which are pregnant with meaning:
" We shall never have any rest. The present is perpetual."
" Art is made to disturb; science reassures."
" Action is a series of desperate acts which allow one to retain hope."
" Emotion is neither an addition nor an imitation. It is the bud of which the work is the flower."

That is how Braque paints. With fervor! The fervor is not spontaneous or a gratuitous act, but a contemplation which slowly realizes itself. It is not a ritual prayer repeated endlessly in the same words, but rather an emotional offering, a gift of onself which asks nothing in return, the joy of rebirth with each work begun, continued and completed. That is Braque's spiritual secret, and it is there that his power lies. It is not a power of shock but of persuasion.

OUR grateful thanks go first of all to Georges Braque, who encouraged us in our work, decided our choice of pictures and opened for us his files and sketchbooks. And he will join us, we feel sure, in thanking Mademoiselle Mariette Lachaud for the vital part she played in the making of this book.

We owe a debt of gratitude to the Galleries which have done so much to make Braque's work better known, in particular to M. Daniel H. Kahnweiler, one of the very first to appreciate its full value, to Madame Louise Leiris, to M. Paul Rosenberg whose photographic archives we found a precious aid, and to MM. Maeght for their unfailing good will in giving us access to the invaluable documentary material in their possession.

The illustration of this book has only been made possible by the friendly cooperation of André Held and Maurice Routhier, the one making available his very complete file of photographs, the other enabling us to benefit once again from his expert knowledge of color reproduction and his extensive collection of ektachromes.

We also take pleasure in extending our thanks to collectors in the United States, Great Britain, Switzerland and France, to Mr. Chester Dale, Mr. Samuel A. Marx, Mr. Walter P. Chrysler Jr., M. Jean de Menil; M. Jacques Dubourg, M. Pierre Levy; Mme Marie Cuttoli, Mme Katia Granoff, Mrs. Edward Hulton, Mrs. Lee Miller Penrose and Mme Sacher, as well as to the Curators of the Art Institute of Chicago, the Museum of Modern Art, New York, the National Gallery of Art, Washington, and The Phillips Collection, Washington, and to MM. Jean Cassou and Bernard Dorival, Curators of the Musée d'Art Moderne, Paris, and M. André Chamson, Curator of the Musée du Petit Palais, Paris.

Messanges 1953.   Paris 1956.

PLATES

Vers 1900-1902
La Grand'mère de l'artiste
Appartient à l'artiste

1

Vers 1900
La Cousine Johanet
Collection Madame Johanet

Vers 1905
BATEAU DANS LE PORT DU HAVRE 3
Collection privée

1905-1906

4 PORT D'ANVERS : LE BATEAU BLANC
Photo Leiris

1907
LA CIOTAT
Paris, Collection D.H. Kahnweiler

6

1905-1906

8 ANVERS : LES BATEAUX PAVOISÉS
Bâle, Kunstmuseum

1907
10 FEMME ASSISE DE DOS
Paris, Collection D.H. Kahnweiler

1907
GRAND NU
Paris, Collection Madame Marie Cuttoli

11

1908
MAISONS A L'ESTAQUE
Berne, Collection M. et Mme Hermann Rupf

12

1908
13 Viaduc a l'Estaque
Photo Leiris

1908-1909
LA ROCHE-GUYON : LE DONJON
Paris, Collection Roger Dutilleul

14

1909
15 BARQUES DE PÊCHE
Collection particulière

1908
COMPOTIER DE FRUITS
Stockholm, Collection Rolf de Maré

19

1909
GUITARE ET COMPOTIER
Berne, Collection M. et Mme Hermann Rupf

20

1910
21   JEUNE FILLE A LA MANDOLINE
Collection Walter P. Chrysler, Jr.

1910
BROC ET VIOLON
Bâle, Kunstmuseum

23

1910
LE SACRÉ-CŒUR
Paris, Collection Roger Dutilleul

24

1910
LA MANDORE
Londres, Collection Mrs Lee Miller Penrose

1911
LE PORTUGAIS
Bâle, Kunstmuseum

26

1911
GUÉRIDON
Paris, Musée National d'Art Moderne

27

1910
NATURE MORTE AU MÉTRONOME   **28**
Photo Leiris

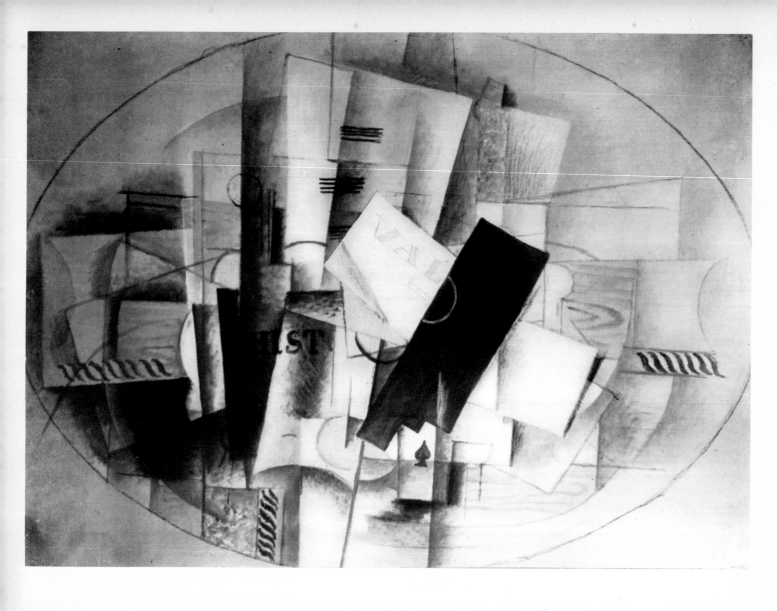

29 1912-1913
NATURE MORTE AVEC PARTITION
Bâle, Kunstmuseum

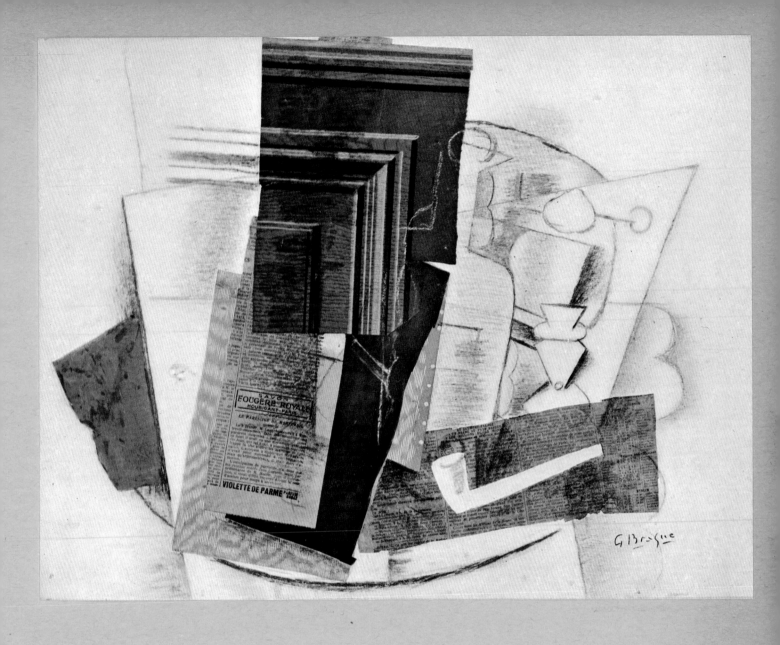

Vers 1914
PAPIER COLLÉ : VIOLETTE DE PARME   **30**
Londres, Collection Mrs Edward Hulton

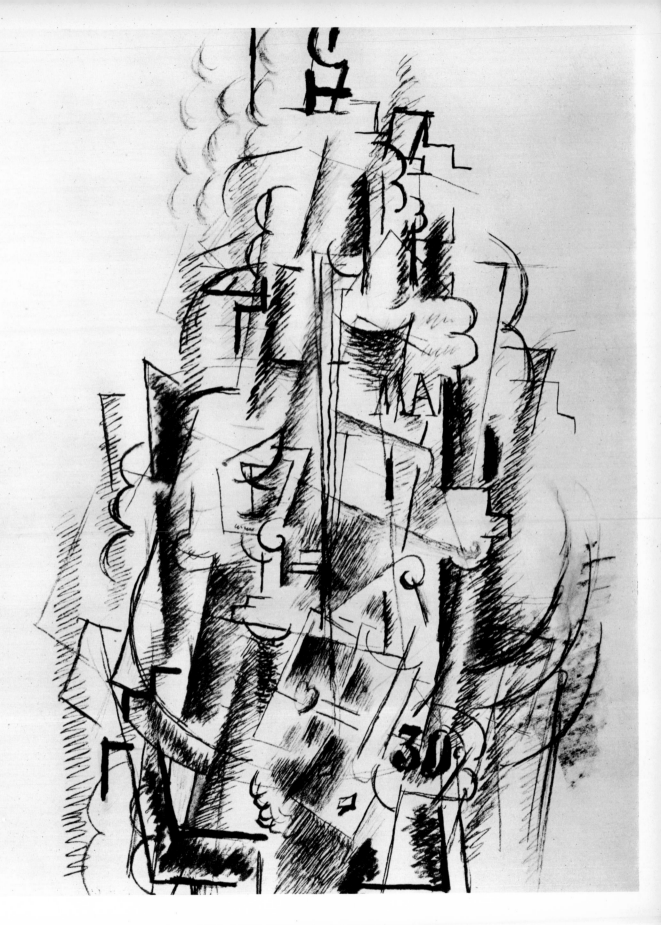

1914
La Bouteille de marc
Dessin à l'encre de Chine

31

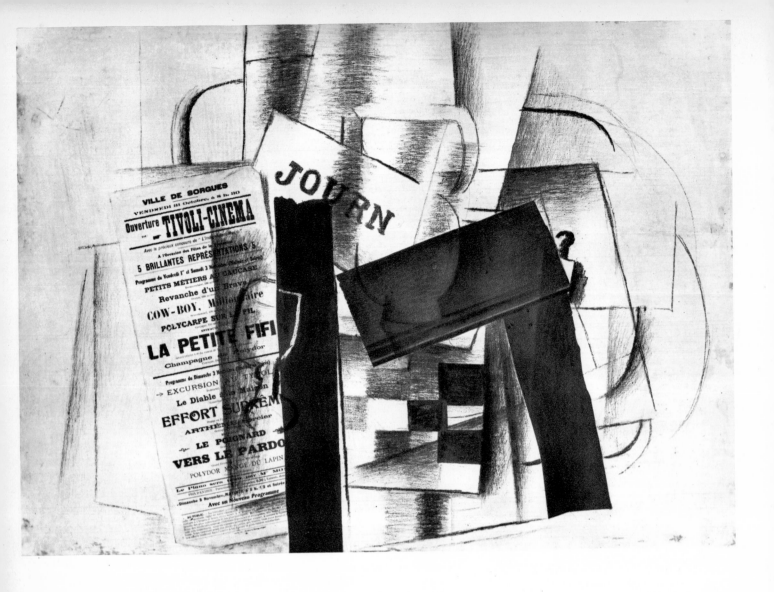

1913
32 PAPIER COLLÉ : TIVOLI-CINÉMA
Photo Leiris

1914
ARIA DE BACH
Paris, Collection Madame Marie Cuttoli

33

1917
34 FEMME A LA MANDOLINE
Paris. Collection Roger Dutilleul

35   LA GUITARISTE
      Bâle, Kunstmuseum

1917

1911-1913
NATURE MORTE AU JEU DE CARTES   **36**
Paris, Musée National d'Art Moderne

37　　1918-1919
La Guitare
Otterlo, Musée Kröller-Müller

Vers 1917
GUITARE
Photo Routhier

38

1914
39 Le Violon
Photo Leiris

40   1919
CAFÉ-BAR
Bâle, Kunstmuseum

1920
NATURE MORTE AVEC POLKA
Hollywood, Collection Mr. et Mrs Walter Arensberg

42 **1922-1923**
ÉTUDE DE NU
Pastel

1923
CANÉPHORE
Ancienne Collection Baron Gourgaud

44

1926
CANÉPHORE
New York, Coll. Chester Dale

45

1924

FEMME NUE COUCHÉE
Photo Bignou-Cooper

46

1925
47 NU ASSIS AU PANIER DE FRUITS
Photo Paul Rosenberg

1924
NU ASSIS AU PANIER DE FRUITS
Santa Barbara, Cal., Collection Whright Hundinglon

48

1923
CHEMINÉE
Photo Paul Rosenberg

49

1922
CHEMINÉE
Chicago, Coll. Samuel A. Marx

50

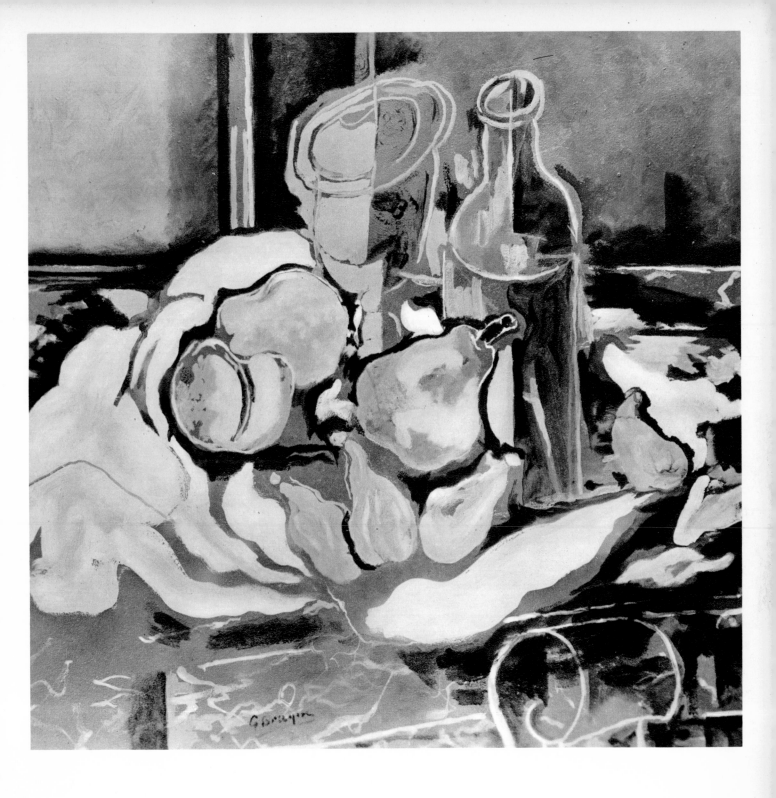

1924
52 NATURE MORTE AVEC PARTITION
Photo Paul Rosenberg

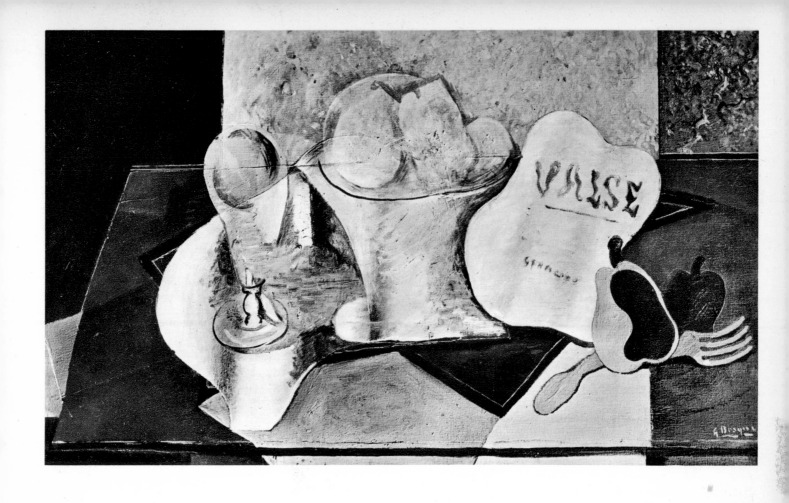

NATURE MORTE A LA VALSE **53**
Photo Paul Rosenberg

G. BRAQUE

1927
GUÉRIDON
Photo Paul Rosenberg

54

1929
LA TABLE RONDE
Washington, Phillips Gallery

55

1926
LE GUÉRIDON
New York, Museum of Modern Art

56

57

1927
LA ROSE NOIRE
Meriden. Conn.. Coll. Mrs Burton Tremaine, Jr.

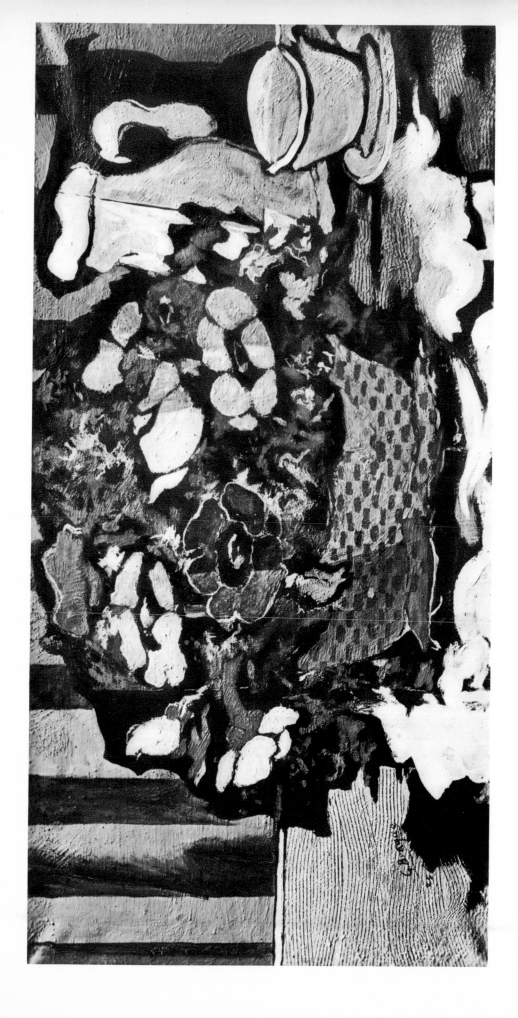

1925
ANÉMONES
U.S.A., Collection particulière

58

1918
GUÉRIDON
Bâle, Kunstmuseum

59

1929
NATURE MORTE AVEC LE JOUR
New York, Collection Chester Dale

1925 — Nature morte
sur table de marbre vert
Paris, Musée d'Art Moderne

61

1928
62 LE PAQUET DE TABAC
Photo Paul Rosenberg

1929
CITRONS
Paris, Collection Jacques Dubourg

63

1932
JOUEUSES DE TENNIS **64**
Appartient à l'artiste

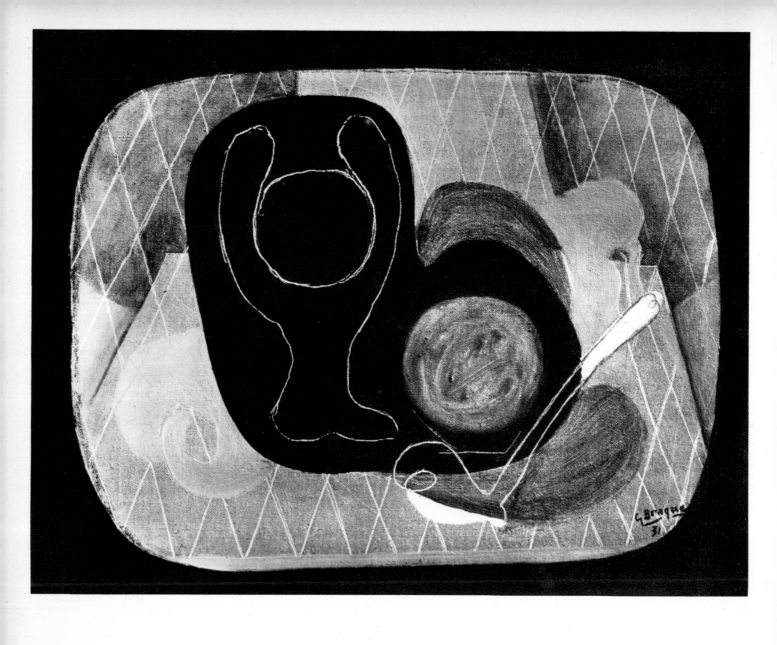

1931
LA PIPE EN TERRE
New York, Museum of Modern Art

65

1929
TÊTE DE FEMME
Photo Paul Rosenberg

67

1928. Falaises et barques
au-dessous : Dessin des Carnets (1949)

68

1929. Cabine, barques, galets
au-dessous : Dessin des Carnets

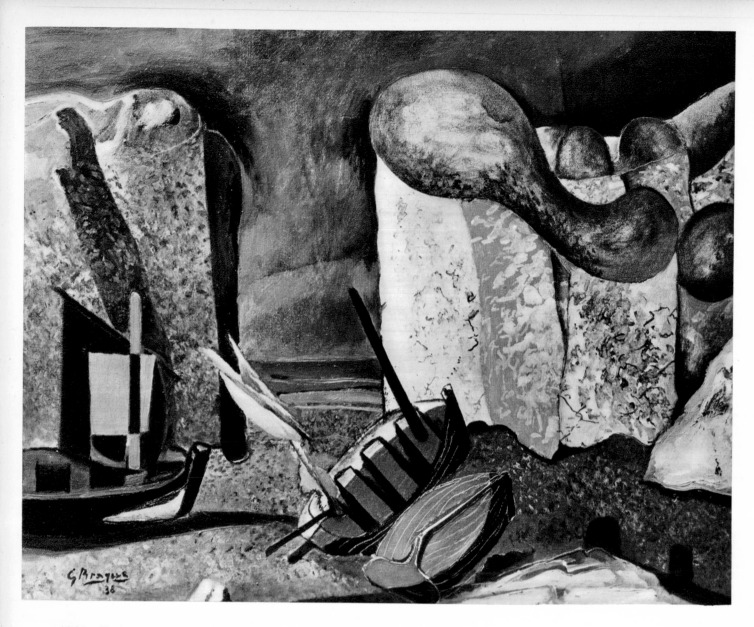

1938. FALAISES
Collection Leigh Bloch, Chicago
au-dessous : Dessin des Carnets

1930
ÉTRETAT
Photo Routhier

1930
BAIGNEUSE II
Photo Routhier

1932-1951
Nu couché (Baigneuse IX)
Appartient à l'artiste

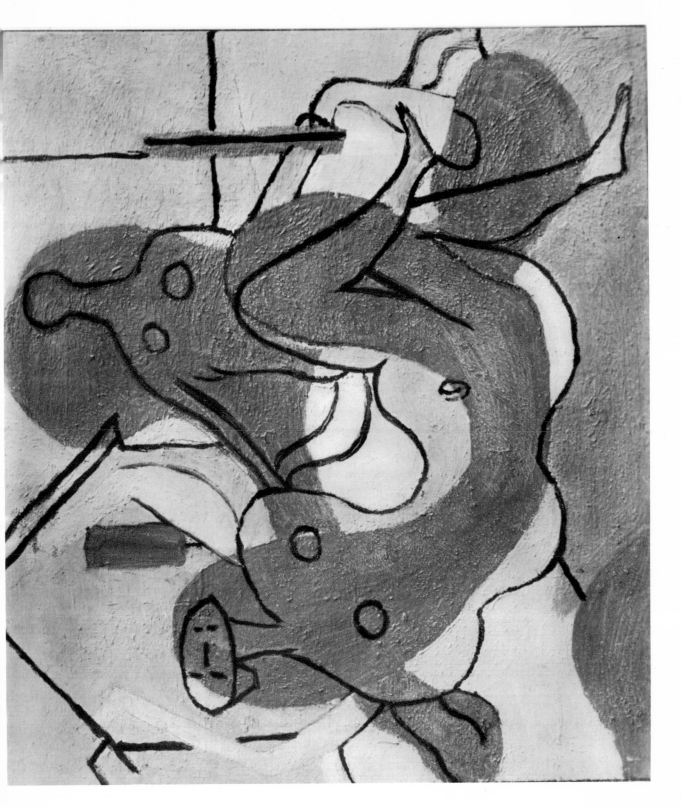

1930-1931
BAIGNEUSE V
Photo Routhier

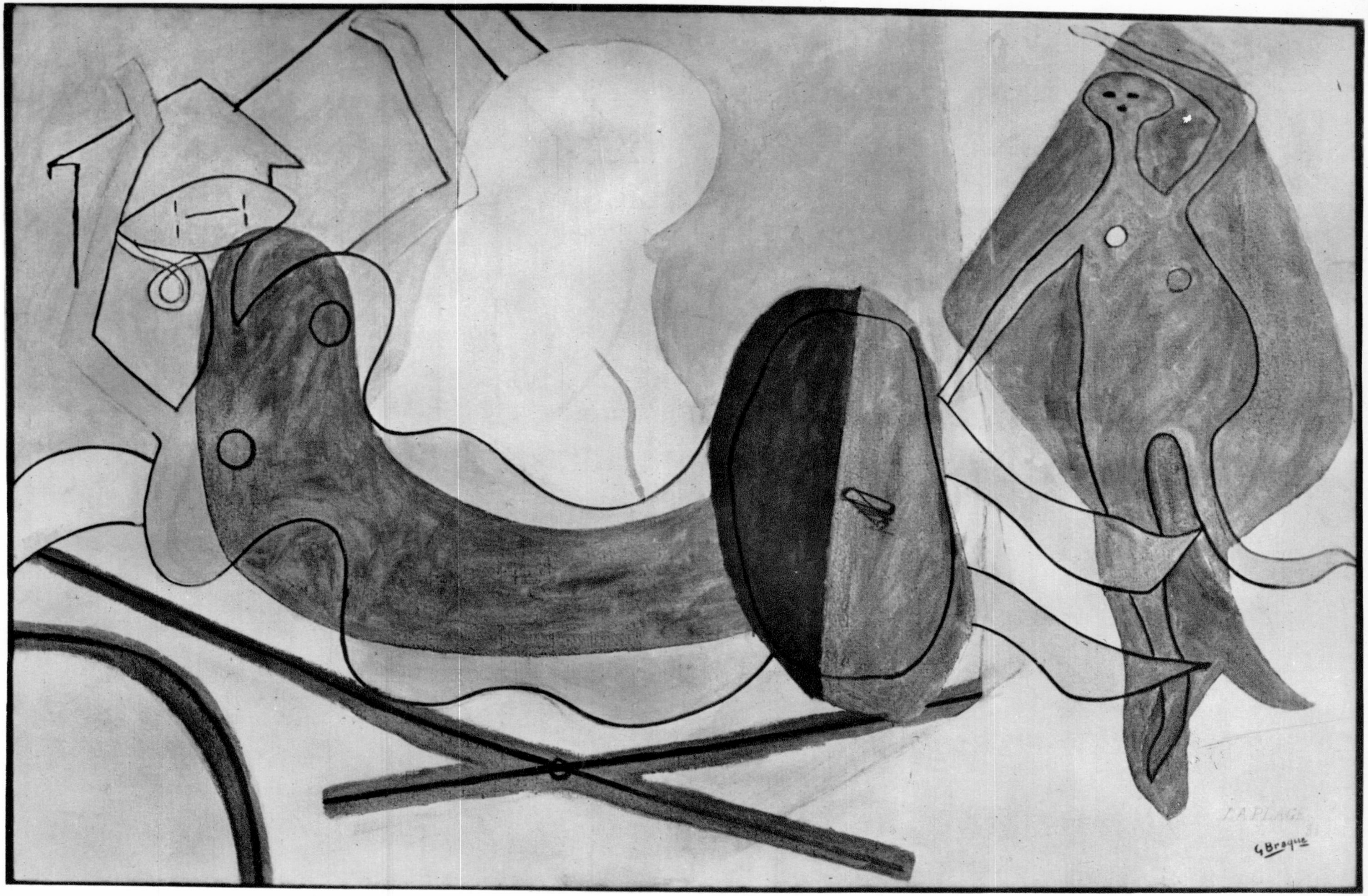

1931
BAIGNEUSE VII
Photo Routhier

76

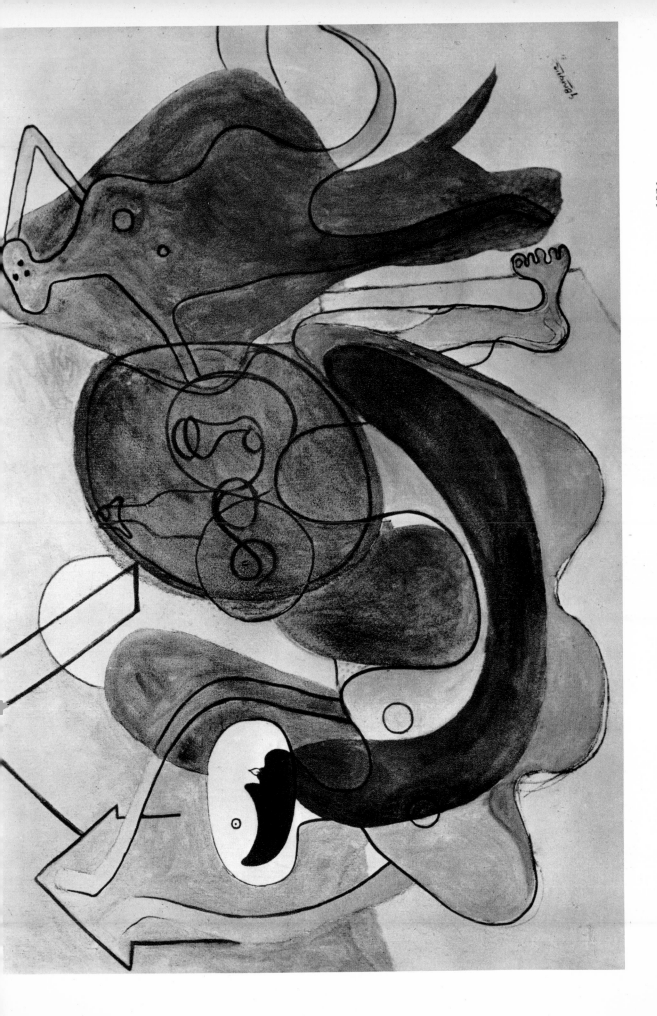

77

1931
BAIGNEUSE VIII
Collection *Walter P. Chrysler, Jr.*

1930
GUÉRIDON AVEC
BOUTEILLE DE MARC
Collection particulière

78

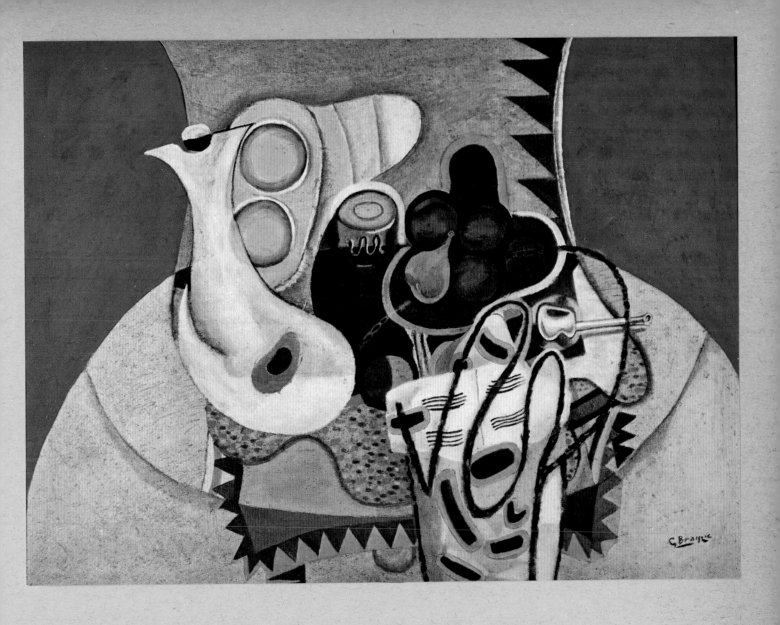

1930
GUÉRIDON
Photo Paul Rosenberg

1934
81 NATURE MORTE : POMMES SUR UN GUÉRIDON
Wayzata, Collection Richard S. Davies

1932
Nature morte   **82**
Suisse, Collection particulière

1933
83 NATURE MORTE AVEC LE SOIR
Photo Routhier

1935
LA NAPPE JAUNE
Chicago, Collection Samuel A. Marx

1936-1937
88   LA MANDOLINE
Chicago, Collection Leigh Bloch

1937
<small>Femme a la Mandoline</small>
New York, Museum of Modern Art

89

1936
FEMME AU CHEVALET
Chicago, Collection Nathan Cummings

91   1937
         FEMME AU CHAPEAU
      Chicago, Collection Samuel A. Marx

1936
LA FEMME-PEINTRE
Paris, Coll. Madame Jacqueline Delubac

93

1937
LE DUO
Paris, Musée National d'Art Moderne

94

1939
LE STUDIO
New York, Collection Paul Rosenberg

95

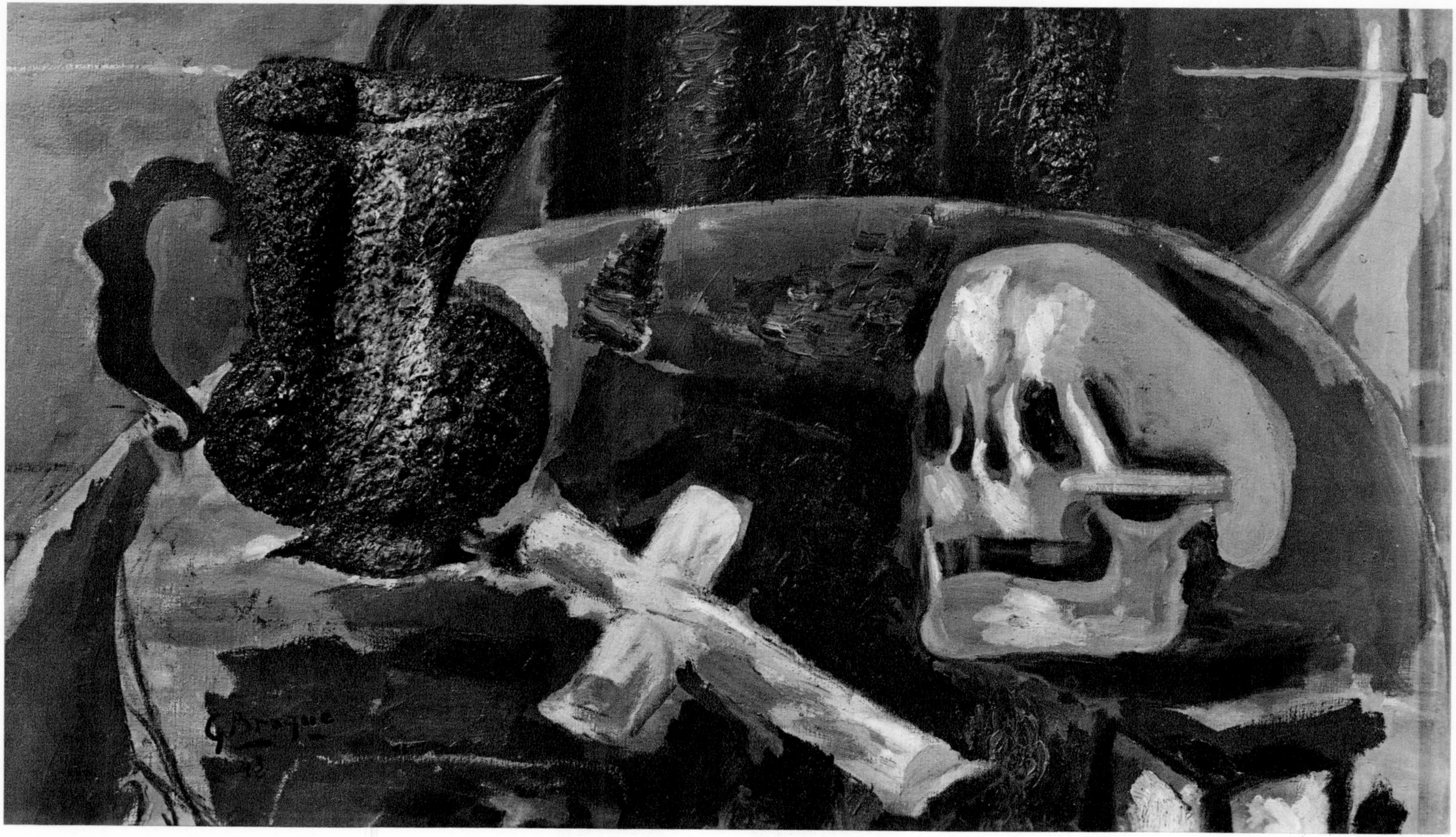

1943
PICHET ET CRANE
Photo Routhier

1942
PICHET, VERRE ET CITRONS
Collection particulière

98

1939
100 LE VERRE DE VIN
Photo Paul Rosenberg

101

LES POISSONS NOIRS
Paris, Musée National d'Art Moderne

1942
NU A LA TOILETTE 103
Photo Routhier

1942
104 DOUBLE FIGURE
Photo Routhier

1942
LA CUVETTE BLEUE
New York, Collection Mr. et Mrs Abner Goldstone

106

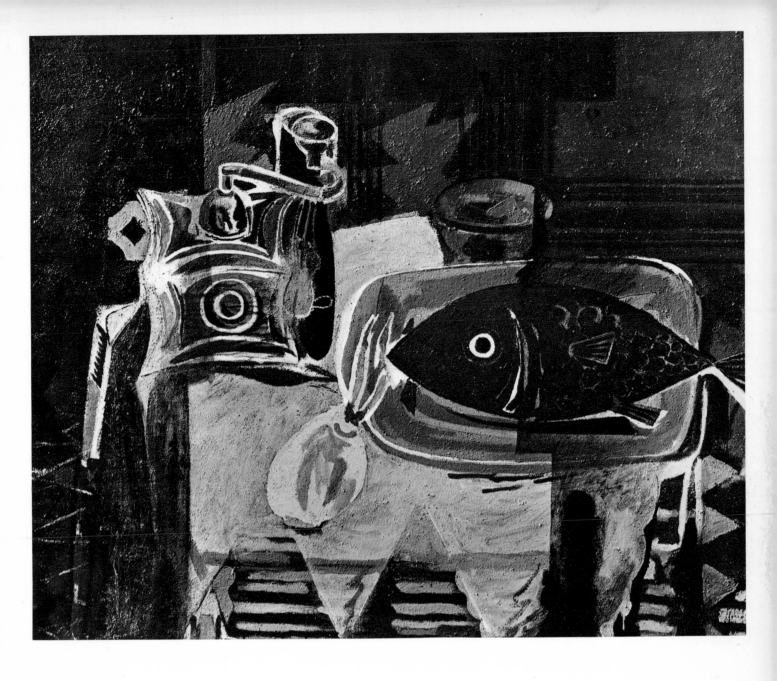

1943
108 LA GUITARE BLEUE
Photo Routhier

1942
INTÉRIEUR : PALETTE ET POT DE FLEURS
U. S. A., collection particulière

1943-1944
LE POÊLE
Photo Roulhier

111

1944
LE SALON
Paris, Musée National d'Art Moderne

1943
LA NAPPE VERTE
Paris, Musée National d'Art Moderne

113

1942
LA CUISINE
Paris, Coll. Jean Paulhan

114

1943
TOURNESOLS
Paris, Collection Madame Jacqueline Delubac

1946
TOURNESOLS
New York, Collection Reader's Digest

1944-1952
LE BILLARD
Mexico, Collection Gelman

117

1945
LA TOILETTE AUX CARREAUX VERTS
Photo Routhier

119

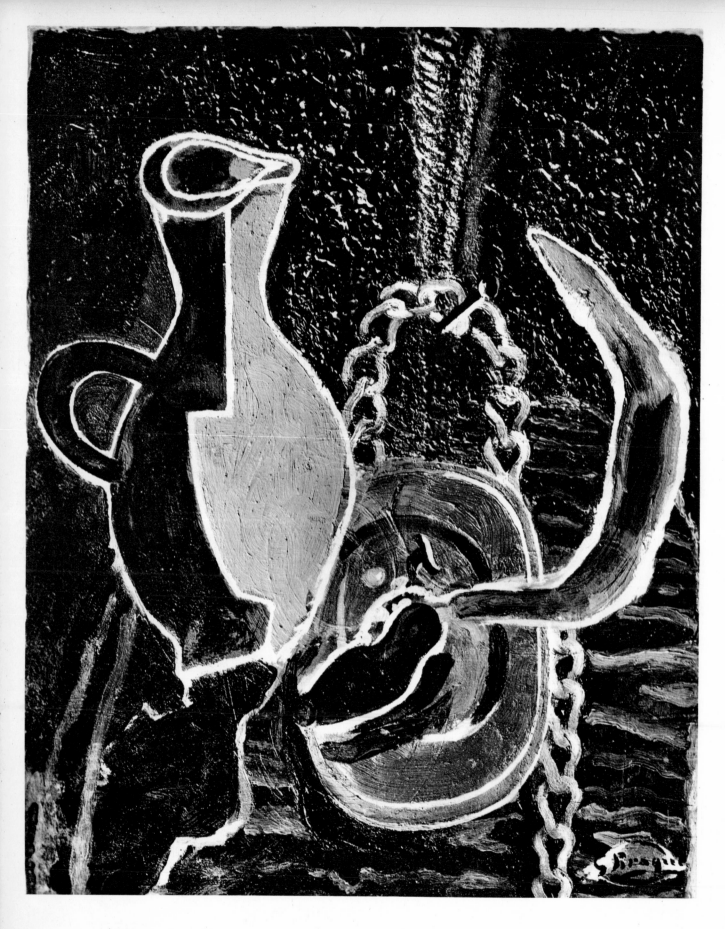

1944
120 La Faucille
Photo Routhier

1952
LE CHAR DU SOLEIL
Zurich, Collection Gustave Zumsteg

1952
123 Double nature morte aux fleurs
Photo Roulhier

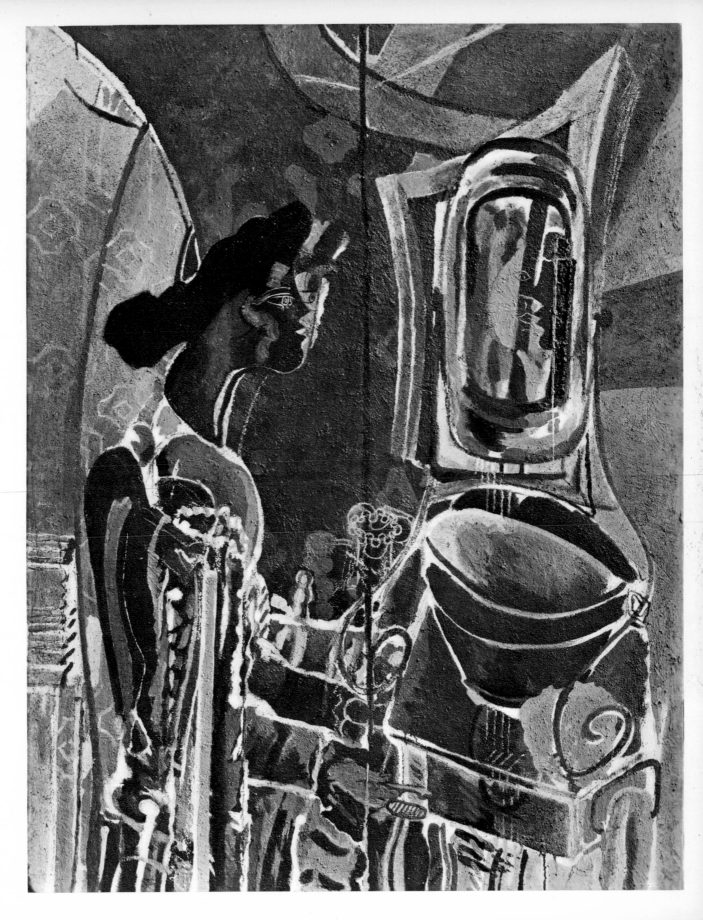

1946
LA FEMME AU MIROIR
Paris, Collection Valentine Dudensing

124

125
1948
LA CAISSE
Photo Routhier

1947
LA CHAISE 126
Appartient à l'artiste

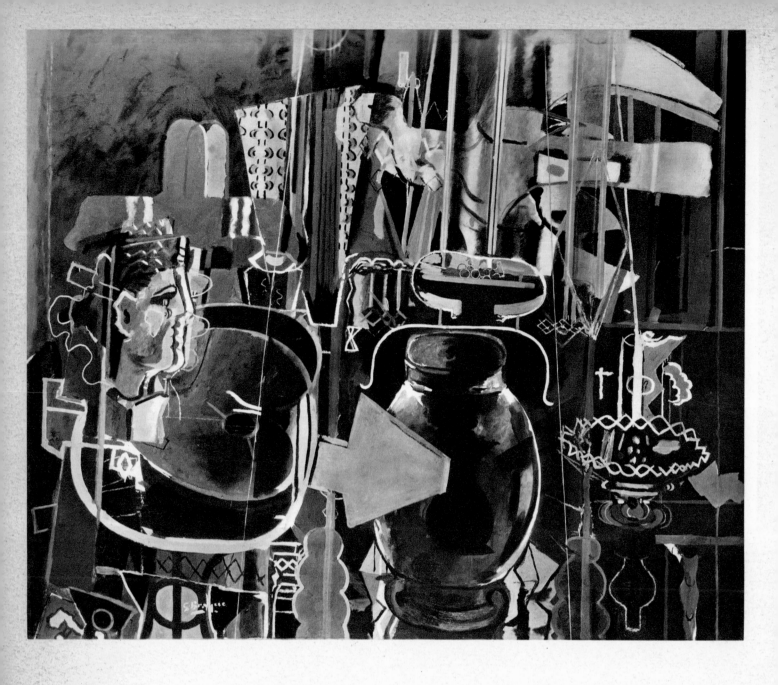

131   1949-1952
ATELIER (VI)
Paris, Galerie Maeght

1954-1955
ATELIER (VIII)
Argilliers, Collection Douglas Cooper

132

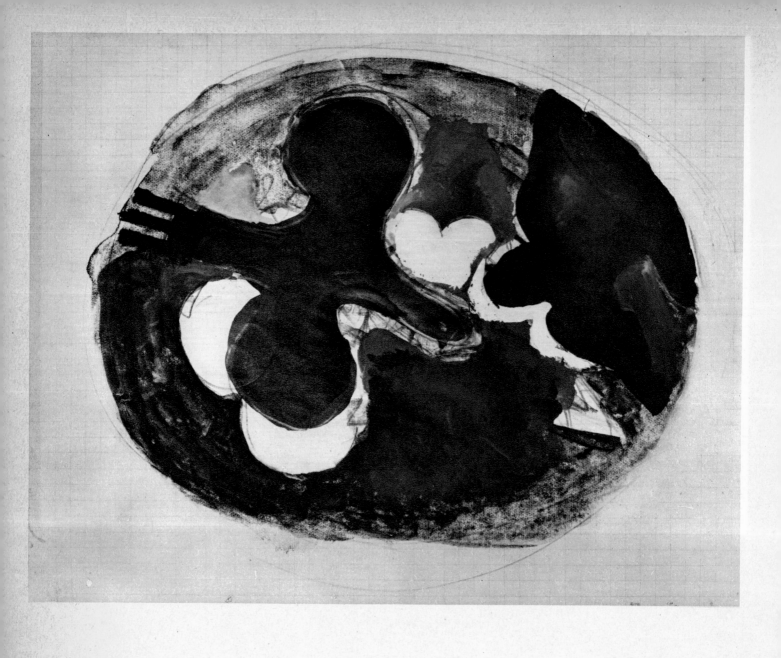

1952
133 ESQUISSE POUR LE PLAFOND DU LOUVRE
Gouache des Carnets

1955
A TIRE D'AILE   **134**
Appartient à l'artiste

1949-1954
AJAX
Collection privée, U.S.A.

TEXTS
ANALYTICAL NOTICES
BIBLIOGRAPHY

REFLECTIONS

Nature does not give us the taste for perfection, we can imagine her as neither better nor worse.
Emotion can neither be added nor imitated. It is the bud, the work is the flower.
Let us be content to induce reflection and not try to convince.

Art is made to disturb. Science reassures.
I do not do what I want, I do what I can.
One must not imitate what one wants to create.
In art there is only one thing valuable: that which cannot be explained.
I am for the rule which corrects the emotion.
Each state is always complementary to the state preceding it.
The painter thinks in forms and colors, his object is poetic creation.

Impregnation — Obsession — Hallucination.

If a painter does not despise painting, he should be afraid of making a picture of greater value than himself.
The artist is not misunderstood, he is underestimated. People exploit him without knowing who he is.
All things considered I prefer those who exploit me to those who follow me. The former have something to teach me.

Reality: *It is not enough to make visible what one paints, it must also be made* touchable.
Visual space — Tactile space:
— Visual space *separates objects one from another.*
— Tactile space *separates us from objects.*
V.S.: The tourist looks at the site.
T.S.: The gunner hits *the target (the trajectory is the prolongation of the arm). True tactile measurements: the foot, the cubit, the thumb...*
When a still life is not within reach of the hand, it ceases to be a still life.

Look for what is in common but not similar. Thus a poet can say that a swallow stabs the sky and turn a swallow into a dagger.
What is in common is true. What is similar is false. Trouillebert resembles Corot, but they have nothing in common.

The painter must not try to remake a story but to bring about a "pictorial fact."
I want to put myself in unison with nature, much more than to copy it.
To discover a thing is to bare it to the quick.
Climate. One must reach a certain temperature which makes things malleable.
Form and color must not be confused together. There must be a simultaneity.
The subject: A lemon next to an orange ceases to be a lemon and the orange an orange, for them both to become fruits. Mathematicians follow this law. So do we.

Limited means give birth to new forms, invite creation and make a style.
To write is not to describe.   To paint is not to depict.   Verisimilitude is no more than
*   illusion.*

Truth exists—only falsehood has to be invented.
Conformity begins with definition.
One cannot always have one's hat in one's hand; hence the hat-stand.
For myself I have found in painting a nail on which to hang my ideas, which allows me
*   to change them and avoid any idée fixe.*
To defend an idea is to take an attitude.
The pessimist does not protect his ideas, he exposes them.
Idealism is a conventional form of Hope.

Have a free mind.   Omnubile concepts.   It was not as a result of profound meditation
*   that man drank from the hollow of his hand (and from the hand to the glass by way of*
*   the shell).   That is more of a metamorphosis than a metaphor.*
Be free in mind, be present.
Few people can say : I am here.   They look for themselves in the past and see themselves
*   in the future.*
I am not a revolutionary painter.   I do not seek for exaltation.   I find fervor sufficient.
Never belong to anything.
With those who cultivate themselves, convictions take the place of faith.

With age, art and life become one.

CHRONOLOGY

1882   May 13, Georges Braque is born at Argenteuil (Seine). His grandfather, his father Charles, and his mother Augustine Johanet, are natives of Argenteuil. He has one sister. They live in the grandfather's house in the rue de l'Hôtel-Dieu. The grandfather is proprietor of a painting business.

1890   The whole family moves to Le Havre, 33, rue Jules Lausne. Charles Braque starts a business for the painting of apartments. Georges Braque enters the Lycée in 1893. In the evenings he studies at the Ecole des Beaux-Arts, where his professor is M. Courchet.

1899   He is 17. His father takes him into the business with him, where he stays a short time. He works for Roncy, a painter and decorator, and continues to study at the Ecole des Beaux-Arts. He begins to paint in oils and learns to play the flute with Gaston Dufy, the brother of Raoul, whom he also knows.

1900   At the end of the year he comes to Paris and continues his apprenticeship as a painter-decorator with Laberthe. He lives in the rue des Trois-Frères in Montmartre, and takes the Municipal Art Course at Les Batignolles, directed by Guignolet. He takes up boxing.

1901-1904   He does his military service near Le Havre. When free, he returns to Paris and lives in the rue Lepic. He signs on at the Académie Humbert, Boulevard Rochechouart, where he meets Picabia and Marie Laurencin. In the fall he presents himself at the Ecole des Beaux-Arts and is accepted by Léon Bonnat in his studio. where there are already two friends of his from Le Havre, Othon Friesz and Raoul Dufy. But at the end of two months he abandons Bonnat's teaching and returns to the Académie Humbert. He passes the summer of 1904 at Honfleur.

> Circa 1900. *Portrait of his grandmother* and of his *Cousin Johanet.*
> 1904. *Garden at Honfleur* (Havre Museum).

1905-1906   He makes friends with the sculptor Manolo and Maurice Raynal. He rents a studio in the rue d'Orsel, in front of the Théâtre Montmartre. He frequents the Louvre Museum and, through Durand-Ruel and Vollard, gets to know the works of the Impressionists. During the summer of 1905 he lives at Quimperlé and Le Havre. In 1906 he goes to Antwerp with Othon Friesz.

> 1905. *Views of the port of Le Havre.*
> 1906. *Views of the Scheldt; Boats in the port of Antwerp.*

This is Braque's Fauve period. He exhibits in 1906 at the Salon des Indépendants and spends the winter at L'Estaque.

1907   New exhibition at the Indépendants. He spends the summer at La Ciotat and the fall at L'Estaque. He changes his manner of painting and turns toward stylization. He makes the acquaintance of Picasso, with whom he has had a faithful and reciprocated friendship ever since. He sees *Les Demoiselles d'Avignon.*

> 1907. *Landscapes at L'Estaque and La Ciotat* (Fauve).

93

1908   Summer and fall at L'Estaque. He undergoes the influence of Cézanne. His pictures are refused by the Salon d'Automne. In November he exhibits at the Galerie Kahnweiler, rue Vignon. Guillaume Apollinaire writes the preface to the catalogue. (It is after having seen the *Houses at L'Estaque* that Louis Vauxcelles writes in *Gil Blas* of "geometrical diagrams, cubes.")

> 1908. *Houses on the hill; Landscapes at L'Estaque* (Cézannesque). *Large Standing Nude.*
> *Still Life with musical instruments* (The Guitar).

1909   He exhibits at the Salon des Indépendants. He spends the summer in La Roche-Guyon; stays at Le Havre and visits the small Norman ports.

> 1909. *La Roche-Guyon and the tower* (Two versions; Coll. R. Dutilleul);
> *Fishing smacks; Port in Normandy; The Fisherman's wife* (Coll. Girardin)
> *Jug, Bottle and Lemon; Guitar and Fruit Dish; The Metronome.*

1910   Beginning of Cubism called "Analytical." Braque has his studio in the rue Caulaincourt. He spends the summer at L'Estaque. He paints his first oval-shaped canvases.

> 1910. *Jug and Violin; The Match-holder; The Mandora; Girl with Mandolin,* oval. (Coll. W.P. Chrysler). *The Sacré-Cœur seen from the studio;*
> 1910. *First engravings* (Kahnweiler): *Job; Fox; Bass; Pal.*

1911   Braque introduces painted lettering in his pictures. The summer he is at Céret with Picasso. This period is common to Braque and Picasso.

1912   During the summer of 1912 he is at Sorgues (Vaucluse) with Pierre Reverdy and Picasso. He introduces *papiers collés* into his pictures. He paints his first picture on a sand foundation and paints imitation woods in trompe-l'œil. Appearance of the playing card theme.

> 1911. *Soda* (round canvas); *Still Life with grapes* (sand foundation); *The Waltz* (oval form).
> *The Guitarist* (Museum of Modern Art); *Le Portugais* (Coll. Laroche, Basel Museum).
> *Le Guéridon* (Musée d'Art Moderne).
> 1913. Papiers collés : LE COURRIER (Philadelphia Museum); *The Clarinet (with lettering* L'ECHO D'A), papier collé and imitation wood; *Still Life with playing cards (The Ace of Clubs)*, gouache and papier collé; TIVOLI CINEMA; VIOLETTE DE PARME (Coll. Mrs. Hulton); TERRE D'EPOUVANTE, etc... *The Musician's Table* (with lettering); *Woman with Guitar* (with the letters LE RÉVEIL), etc...

1914-1915   Braque is mobilized with the rank of sergeant in the 224th Infantry. Wounded at Carency he has to be trepanned. Twice mentioned in dispatches.

> 1914. *The Violin* (oval) *with lettering* DUO; *Violin and Glass* (pointillist); *Composition with the lettering* JOH; Papier collé : *Aria de Bach.*

1916-1917   Convalescent and invalided out (1916). He soon begins to paint again. He uses large flat tints. Stays again at Sorgues.

> 1917. *Woman with Mandolin; La Musicienne* (Basel Museum).

1918-1919   Braque inaugurates a new Cubism. In March 1919 he exhibits at Léonce Rosenberg's, in "L'Effort Moderne."

> 1918. *Still Life with Guitar* (in a diamond) (M. Kröller-Müller); *The Goblet: A Mr. Gaaltin* (in an octagon); *La Bouteille de rhum* (vertical oval) (Coll. J. Pulitzer); *Clarinet with lettering* LE RAD (oval in breadth) (Basel Museum); *First Guéridon* (Basel Museum).
> 1919. *On the table* (sand foundation).
> 1919. *Café-Bar* (Coll. Laroche, Basel Museum).

94

1920-1924 The year 1920 marks the beginning of a new manner.   In 1922 he exhibits at the Salon d'Automne.   In 1924 first exhibition at Paul Rosenberg's.

> 1920. *Guitar with lettering* RHUM (on plaster); *Guitar and lettering* POLKA.
> First sculpture: *Figure of standing woman* (plaster).
> 1922-23. *First Cheminées* (continuing until 1927).
> 1923-24. *Canéphorae; Seated nude with basket of fruit.*

1925-1932 In 1924 Braque leaves the rue Caulaincourt where he has worked for 15| years, and moves to the Avenue Reille where he stays for two years (1924-1925).   In 1926 he moves for good into the house built for him by Auguste Perret, 6, rue du Douanier, at the Parc Montsouris. Toward 1927 the tones he uses are noticeably more lively.   In 1927 and again in 1929 he spends the summer at Dieppe.

> Numerous still Lifes: *Still Life with Waltz* (1926) *The Black Rose* (1927); *Still Life with* LE JOUR (1929), etc... Flowers: *Anemones* (1925), several versions.
> 1927-30. Series of *Guéridons; Still Life on the table* (Musée d'Art Moderne)
> 1928. *Athena* (lithograph in 1932).
> 1929. *Studies for Double head of a Woman.*
> 1929-30. *Beaches; Cliffs; Fishing Boats; Shingle.*
> 1930-31. Series of *Baigneuses.*
> 1930. *The Blue Mandolin* (first version).
> 1931. *The Red Tablecloth* (Coll. Mrs. Edna K. Wartner).

1933 At the end of 1932, travels in Switzerland.   In April 1933, at Basel large exhibition of Braque's work (183 items).   Special number of *Cahiers d'Art* and publication of Carl Einstein's book.

> 1932. *Engraved plasters* on black foundation.
> 1933. *The Pink Tablecloth; Still Life with* LE SOIR (plaster foundation).

1935-1939 Travels in Germany in 1936.   1936-1939 Braque uses figures with a double face in his interiors. In 1937 *The Yellow Tablecloth*, painted in 1935, is awarded the first prize by the Carnegie Foundation at Pittsburgh.

In 1939, at the beginning of the war, Braque sculpts on rock.   He also models in plaster.

> 1935-37. *Figures in composition* (double faces).
> 1935. *The Yellow Tablecloth* (Coll. Samuel A. Marx, Chicago).
> 1938. *Cliffs* (Coll. Leigh Bloch, Chicago).
> 1939. *Vanitas.*
> 1936. *Mandolin* (Coll. Leigh Bloch, Chicago).

1940-1944 Braque retires to the Limousin, then to the Pyrenees.   In 1944 only he returns to Varengeville.

1945 Travels to Brussels.   Braque exhibitions at Brussels, then at Amsterdam.   He is made officer of the Legion of Honor.

> 1939-40. *The Studio* (Coll. Paul Rosenberg).
> 1940. *Bread and Jug;* 1941, *Bread.*
> 1942. *Black Fish; Brown Fish* (Musée d'Art Moderne).
> *The Blue Basin; The Green Basin.*
> *Double Figure against sea background.*
> *Pictures with vertical form: La Toilette devant la Fenêtre* (two versions):
> *Le Poêle; The Kitchen* (Coll. Jean Paulhan).
> 1942. *Patience.*
> 1943. *Green Carpets* (two versions); *Sunflowers; The Coffee Mill and the Fish; Jug and Skull; The Blue Guitar* (second version).
> 1944. *The Salon* (Musée d'Art Moderne); *The Sickle; The Pumpkin.*

1945-1947 Braque once more uses the X construction begun in 1942 with *Three Lemons* (Pl. 98) and the *Green Carpet* of 1943.   This time it is *Billiards*.   He produces the first lithographs,

Helios. In 1946 he exhibits in London. In 1946 first large exhibition at the Galerie Maeght in Paris; Maeght publishes the "*Cahiers de Braque 1946-1947.*"

1945. *Billiards* (three versions).
1946. *Double Still Life with flowers; La Femme au miroir; The Chair; The Packing-case.*
1946-48. *Helios* lithographs.

1948   At the Venice Biennale in 1948, his *Billiards* is awarded first prize. Travels to Venice.

1949-1956   In 1949 comprehensive exhibition of his work at the Museum of Modern Art in New York (114 items.) In 1951 Braque is made commander of the Legion of Honor. It is the period of the *Ateliers* and soon to be that of the *Birds.* In 1952 he is commissioned to paint a ceiling for the Room of Antique Etruscan Art at the Louvre Museum.
In 1955 the "Theogony of Hesiod" appears, published by Maeght; begun in 1930 for Vollard.
A large Braque exhibition at Tokyo in 1952; another very important one at Berne in 1953.
In 1956 he receives a Doctorate *honoris causa* at Oxford University.
General exhibition in Edinburgh and London in preparation for the summer of 1956.

1949-55. Series of *Ateliers.*
1952-53. Ceiling at the Louvre.
1955. Large compositions on a bird theme: *The Bird and its nest; On the Wing.*

ANALYTICAL NOTICES

About 1900-02   1
THE ARTIST'S GRANDMOTHER
Property of the artist.

Ht. 0.61; Wdth. 0.50 meters
  She is wearing a red chenille bonnet.
  Braque has also painted a large portrait of his mother, seated, a portrait entirely inspired by Toulouse-Lautrec, in composition and execution.

About 1900   2
COUSIN JOHANET
Mme Johanet Collection.

Ht. 0.61; Wdth. 0.50.   Also called the Little Girl in Blue.

About 1905   3
BOAT IN THE PORT OF LE HAVRE
Private collection.

1905-06   4
THE PORT OF ANTWERP: THE WHITE BOAT
Signed at bottom left.

1906   5
L'ESTAQUE
Property of the artist.

Ht. 0.60; Wdth. 0.50.   Signed at bottom left and dated 06.
  The painting belongs to Braque's Fauve period.   Painted in dots of color, it is very different in technique from the following picture (Pl. 6).   Braque returned to L'Estaque two years later in 1908, having become a follower of Cézanne.

1907   6
LA CIOTAT
Paris, D.H. Kahnweiler Collection.

Ht. 0.36; Wdth. 0.48.

1905-06   7
ANTWERP: THE MAST

Ht. 0.46; Wdth. 0.38.
  The estuary of the Scheldt at Antwerp.   There exists a study in width in Indian ink, of which only the left hand part appears in the painting.

1905-06   8
ANTWERP: SHIPS DRESSED
Basel, Kunstmuseum (Hoffmann Stiftung).

  Less lively in its tones than Pl. 4 or that in the Baron von der Heydt Collection, Ascona (Switzerland), it shows remnants of the Impressionism with which O. Friesz, who was with Braque at Antwerp, was imbued.

1906   9
LANDSCAPE AT LA CIOTAT
Ht. 0.50; Wdth. 0.61.   Signed at left bottom.   Dated 06.
Paris, D.H. Kahnweiler Collection.

1907   10
WOMAN SEATED, BACK VIEW
Ht. 0.55; Wdth. 0.46.
  There exists a variant (0.60 × 0.50; repr. Hope, p. 22), M. and Mme Jacques Helft Collection, Buenos-Aires.

1907   11
LARGE NUDE
Paris, Mme Marie Cuttoli Collection.

Ht. 1.40; Wdth. 1.00.   Signed at bottom right.
  It is this picture which is said to have been painted under the influence of Picasso's "Les Demoiselles d'Avignon."

1908   12
HOUSES AT L'ESTAQUE
Berne, Hermann Rupf Collection.

Ht. 0.73; Wdth. 0.60.   Signed on the back.
  Going to L'Estaque as a Fauve in 1905-1906, Braque returned in 1908 as a follower of Cézanne.   This picture is one of the most famous in the history of the beginnings of Cubism.   Shown by Kahnweiler (Nov. 9-28, 1908) it occasioned the article of Louis Vauxcelles (*Gil Blas*, Nov. 14, 1908) in which he said: "Braque despises form and reduces everything, figures, sites and houses to geometric diagrams, to little cubes."   Cubism had found its name.

1908   13
VIADUCT AT L'ESTAQUE
Ht. 0.73; Wdth. 0.60.
  The layout reminds one of the ogival frame of Cézanne's "Baigneuses."

1908-09   14
LA ROCHE-GUYON: THE KEEP
Paris, Roger Dutilleul Collection.

Ht. 0.73; Wdth. 0.60.
  The framing reminds one of Cézanne's Gardanne period. There exists a variant in the same collection.   The collector Roger Dutilleul was one of the first to take an interest in Braque (see the *Woman with Mandolin*, Pl. 34, the *Sacré Cœur*, Pl. 24, etc.).

1909   15
FISHING BOATS
Private collection.

Ht. 0.92; Wdth. 0.73.

1908   16
PORT IN NORMANDY
Walter P. Chrysler, Jr. Collection.

Ht. 0.81; Wdth. 0.81.

1909   17
THE TOWN ON THE HILL
Basel, Kunstmuseum.

Ht. 0.81; Wdth. 0.65.

The Cubist construction is more and more apparent, influenced by Cézanne's Gardanne period.

1909   18
STILL LIFE WITH MUSICAL INSTRUMENTS
Property of the artist.

Ht. 0.50; Wdth. 0.61. Signed at left bottom (the signature is of recent date).

This picture is the first of the Cubist period which included musical instruments. After it guitars and mandolins were the themes of many cubist paintings.

The clarinet which figures in the picture appears again in other works of Braque, of Picasso and of André Derain. The music score is also a theme found often later.

1908   19
FRUIT DISH
Stockholm, Rolf de Maré Collection.

Ht. 0.65; Wdth. 0.54.

1909   20
GUITAR AND FRUIT DISH
Berne, Hermann Rupf Collection.

Ht. 0.73; Wdth. 0.60. Signed on the back.
Painted in bluish greens and yellows.

1910   21
GIRL WITH MANDOLIN
Walter P. Chrysler, Jr. Collection.

Oval. Ht. 0.92; Wdth. 0.73. Signed at bottom left.

1909   22
WOMAN'S HEAD
Paris, Musée Municipal des Beaux-Arts.

Ht. 0.44; Wdth. 0.31.
Called the *"Fisherman's Wife."*

1910   23
JUG AND VIOLIN
Basel, Kunstmuseum.

Ht. 1.16; Wdth. 0.81.

1910   24
LE SACRÉ CŒUR
Paris, Roger Dutilleul Collection.

Ht. 0.55; Wdth. 0.41.

View of Montmartre from Braque's studio, rue Caulaincourt (see photo p. 14). Inaugurates the series of windows following the *Window* painted in 1906. There is another painted at Céret, in 1911 (0.46 × 0.38).

1910   25
THE MANDORA
London, Mrs. Lee Miller Penrose Collection.

Ht. 0.73; Wdth. 0.59. Signed on the back.

1911   26
LE PORTUGAIS
Basel, Kunstmuseum.

Ht. 1.16; Wdth. 0.81.

One of the numerous musicians, male or female, painted by Braque and the other Cubist painters. Note the lettering painted in stencil, B A L, C O and the numbers 1040.

1911   27
GUÉRIDON (PEDESTAL TABLE)
Paris, Musée National d'Art Moderne.

Ht. 1.16; Wdth. 0.81.

With a drawing called *A la Bouteille de Marc* Pl. 31, a bottle which is a figuration very dear to Braque—it is the first appearance of the "Guéridon" and "Table" themes and their "Chimney-piece" variants.

1910   28
STILL LIFE WITH METRONOME

Ht. 0.81; Wdth. 0.54.

Related to the *Mandora* (Pl. 25) of which it is a complicated variant. It is called *With Metronome* because this object figures on top and on the left. There exists, of this same year, a picture called *The Metronome* in which the said object is emphasized.

1912-13   29
STILL LIFE WITH MUSIC SCORE
Basel, Kunstmuseum.

Ht. 0.65; Wdth. 0.92.
Also called *"The Musician's Table."*

About 1914   30
PAPIER COLLÉ (VIOLETTE DE PARME)
London, Mrs. Edward Hulton Collection.

Ht. 0.48; Wdth. 0.64. Signed at bottom right.

1914   31
LA BOUTEILLE DE MARC
Drawing in Indian Ink.

Related to Pl. 27.

1913   32
PAPIER COLLÉ (TIVOLI CINEMA)

Ht. 0.65; Wdth. 0.92.

Often related to the *"Statue d'épouvante"*. Tivoli Cinema is a cinema at Sorgues to which Picasso and Braque went together. (La Statue d'épouvante is the title of a film which was shown there.)

1914   33
ARIA DE BACH
Paris, Mme Cuttoli Collection.

Ht. 0.46; Wdth. 0.325. Signed at bottom right.

1917   34
WOMAN WITH MANDOLIN
Paris, Roger Dutilleul Collection.

Ht. 0.92; Wdth. 0.65.

Here we note a return to the reality of the object. The background introduces that of the "Goblet" and similar still lifes of 1917-1918, which may be called *toile d'araignée* (Spider's Web).

1917   35

THE GUITARIST

Basel, Kunstmuseum (Coll. Raoul Laroche).

Ht. 2.20; Wdth. 1.125.   Signed in the middle toward the left.

1911-1913   36

STILL LIFE WITH PLAYING CARDS

Paris, Musée National d'Art Moderne.

Ht. 0.80; Wdth. 0.59.   Also called the *Ace of Clubs.*
The disposition of the figurations in the still life is not particular to this picture.   It is found again in many others of the period, with a bunch of grapes at the top.

1918-1919   37

THE GUITAR

Otterlo, Kröller-Müller Museum.

Ht. 0.60; Wdth. 1.00.
Composition in a diamond.

About 1917   38

THE GUITAR

Toile d'Araignée composition in an octagon; note the pointillism.

1914   39

THE VIOLIN

Pointillist picture with lettering.

1919   40

CAFÉ-BAR

Basel, Kunstmuseum (Coll. Raoul Laroche).

Ht. 1.16; Wdth. 0.73.
Zervos (*Cahiers d'Art* 1933) reproduces another version of this study of *guéridons* (pedestal tables) with the inscription FÉ-BAR, divided by the left edge of the canvas.

1920   41

STILL LIFE WITH POLKA

Hollywood, Mr. and Mrs. Walter Arensberg Collection.

Ht. 0.43; Wdth. 0.92.
Lettering appeared in Braque's work from 1911 on (cf. pl. 26 Le Portugais).   In 1912 RHUM, MARC, ETUDE, VALSE, JOURNAL or names of newspapers.   This lettering is used by him up to the present day.

1922-23   42

NUDE STUDY

Pastel.   Signed at bottom left.

1922-23   43

NUDE STUDY

Pastel.   Signed at bottom left.

1923   44

CANEPHORA

Former Baron Gourgaud Collection.

Ht. 1.805; Wdth. 0.72.   Signed at bottom right.
The picture has a pendant signed at bottom left.

1926   45

CANEPHORA

New York, Chester Dale Collection.

Ht. 1.60; Wdth. 0.73.   Signed at bottom left, dated 26.
Was shown on loan at the Art Institute of Chicago and is now in the National Gallery, Washington.

1924   46

RECUMBENT NUDE WOMAN

New York, Chester Dale Collection.

Signed at bottom left, dated 24.

1925   47

SEATED NUDE WITH BASKET OF FRUIT

Signed at bottom left, dated 25.
Another example, no less fine, is in the National Gallery, Washington (1.00 × 0.81).

1924   48

SEATED NUDE WITH BASKET OF FRUIT

Santa Barbara, Calif., Wright Lundington Collection.

Ht. 0.91; Wdth. 0.73.   Signed at bottom right.

1923   49

CHEMINÉE (Chimney-piece and fire-place)

Ht. 1.63; Wdth. 0.73.   Signed at bottom right, dated 23.
A very close variant, repeating the theme, dated 1927, and of the same dimensions, is reproduced in Hope 101 (signed and dated bottom right 27).   Norton Art Gallery, West Palm Beach, Florida.

1922   50

CHEMINÉE

Chicago, Samuel A. Marx Collection.

Ht. 1.27; Wdth. 0.76.   Signed at bottom right.

1924   51

BOTTLE AND PEARS

1924   52

STILL LIFE WITH MUSIC SCORE

Signed at bottom left, dated 24.

1926   53

STILL LIFE WITH WALTZ

1927   54

GUÉRIDON

Signed at bottom right, dated 27.
The canvas has been completed by the artist with a narrow panel of painted wood, with the name in the large letters used habitually by manufacturers of packing cases.

1929   55

THE ROUND TABLE

Washington, The Phillips Collection.

Ht. 1.47; Wdth. 1.15.   Signed at bottom right.
With lettering ETUDE.
The last version in the *Guéridon* series is one of very recent date (about 1952, property of the artist): *Le Guéridon Rouge,* with a triple iron foot.

1926   56

GUÉRIDON

New York, Museum of Modern Art.

Ht. 1.35; Wdth. 0.73.   Signed at bottom right, and dated 26.

1927   57

THE BLACK ROSE

Meriden, Conn., Mrs. Burton Tremaine, Jr. Collection.

Ht. 0.51; Wdth. 0.94. Signed at bottom left, and dated 27.
 The motif of the rose-tree branch is repeated in several
still lifes. and notably in a closely related composition;
Guitar, Fruit-Dish and Pot (Ht. 0.73; Wdth. 0.91), Mr. and
Mrs. Lincoln M. Schulster Coll., New York.
In a very difficult selection necessitated by the amplitude
of the theme, Braque was represented in the Still Life Exhibition at the Orangerie, 1952, by two works, considered masterpieces in the genre, this *Black Rose* and the *Pink Tablecloth*, Pl. 79.

1925   58

ANEMONES

U.S.A. Private Collection.

Ht. 0.36; Wdth. 0.72. Signed at bottom left, dated 25.
 The bowls of flowers and baskets of fruit become numerous
in the years of experiment of the Canephorae and Nudes
with basket.

1918   59

GUÉRIDON

Basel, Kunstmuseum.

This *guéridon*, clearly contemporary with the two *Café-Bar
guéridons* (one repr. Pl. 40) is distinguished from them and
even more from the *guéridons* of 1927 and 28 (Pls. 54 and 56)
by its backgrounds with superposed planes.

1929   60

STILL LIFE WITH LE JOUR

New York, Chester Dale Collection.

Ht. 1.03; Wdth. 1.60. Signed at bottom right, dated 29.
 Was exhibited on loan in the Art Institute of Chicago
and is now in the National Gallery, Washington.

1925   61

STILL LIFE ON GREEN MARBLE TABLE

Paris, Musée National d'Art Moderne.

Ht. 1.30; Wdth. 0.75. Signed at bottom right, dated 25.

1928   62

THE PACKET OF TOBACCO

Signed at bottom right, dated 28.

1929   63

LEMONS

Paris, Jacques Dubourg Collection.

Ht. 0.33; Wdth. 0.455. Signed at bottom right, dated 29.

1922   64

TENNIS PLAYERS

Property of the artist.

Ht. 0.15; Wdth. 0.21. Pen and wash.
 One notes here, in a sort of Expressionism, unusual enough
and possibly only humorous, the numerous signs indicating
the rapidity of the movements; note the heads forming arrows,
which also characterize a number of etchings inspired by the
chariot theme.

1931   65

THE CLAY PIPE

New York, Museum of Modern Art.

Ht. 0.27; Wdth. 0.35. Signed at bottom right, dated 31.

1929-30   66

LEMONS, NUTS AND TOBACCO JAR

Former Collection Baron Gourgaud.

1929   67

HEAD OF A WOMAN

Signed at bottom left, dated 29.
 Christian Zervos, in the special number of Cahiers d'Art
of 1933, published four female figures. The artist says he
destroyed many of them but spared this one.

1928   68

CLIFFS AND BOATS

Signed at bottom left, dated 28.

1949

ANCHOR, NET, FISH, BASKET

Drawing-book. Crayon.

Ht. 0.13; Wdth. 0.17.

1929   69

CABIN, BOATS, SHINGLE

Signed at bottom left, dated 29.

1937

BOATS

Drawing-book. Crayon.

Ht. 10.5; Wdth. 19.5.

1938   70

CLIFFS

Chicago, Leigh Bloch Collection.

Ht. 0.50;Wdth. 0.65. Signed at bottom left and dated 38.

1937

BOATS AND CLIFFS

Drawing-book. Crayon.

Ht. 0.10; Wdth. 0.15.

1939 (?)   71

BOATS ON THE BEACH

Paris, Katia Granoff Collection.

Ht. 0.30; Wdth. 0.55.

1930   72

ETRETAT

1930   73

BAIGNEUSE (II)

1932-51   74

RECUMBENT NUDE (BAIGNEUSE IX)

Property of the artist.

Ht. 1.12; Wdth. 1.95.

1930-31   75

BAIGNEUSE (V)

1931   76

BAIGNEUSE (VII)

Signed at bottom right, dated, LA PLAGE 31.

100

1931   **77**
BAIGNEUSE (VIII)

Walter P. Chrysler, Jr. Collection.

Ht. 1.30; Wdth. 1.95. Signed at bottom right, dated 31.

In this series, one of the most important in Braque's work, we have eight versions, about the years 1930-1931 (Pls. 73-75-76-77), and a ninth recumbent figure in an interior, which is still in his studio and was only finished in 1951 (Ht. 1.12; Wdth. 1.95; Pl. 74). Finally in the same experimental period, is a Recumbent Woman (1930-1952; H. 0.73; Wdth. 1.80, Property of the artist), remarkable for its multiplication of exterior, curved forms, united in their center to figurations of the *Baigneuse* herself. See text and analysis of pictures pp. 43-45.

1930   **78**
GUÉRIDON AVEC BOUTEILLE DE MARC

New York, Private Collection.

Ht. 1.30; Wdth. 0.73. Signed at bottom left, dated 30.

1933   **79**
THE PINK TABLECLOTH

Walter P. Chrysler, Jr. Collection.

Ht. 0.97; Wdth. 1.30. Signed at bottom right.

1930   **80**
GUÉRIDON

1934   **81**
STILL LIFE: APPLES ON A TABLE

Wayzata, Minnesota, Richard S. Davies Collection.

Ht. 0.505; Wdth. 0.67. Sanguine study. Signed at bottom right.

1932   **82**
STILL LIFE

Switzerland, Private Collection.

1933   **83**
STILL LIFE WITH LE SOIR

On plaster foundation. Signed at bottom right.

1935   **84**
THE YELLOW TABLECLOTH

Chicago, Samuel A. Marx Collection.

Ht. 1.03; Wdth. 1.43. Signed at bottom left.

The picture was awarded the Grand Prix of the Carnegie Foundation in 1937.

1938   **85**
ATELIER WITH STILL LIFE AND LEFT PROFILE

Ht. 0.92; Wdth. 0.33. Signed at bottom right.
Date as given by the artist. Laufer, *op. cit.*, says 1941.

1937   **86**
DOUBLE FIGURE

Drawing-book. Crayon.
Ht. 1.13; Wdth. 0.10.

1937   **87**
DOUBLE FIGURE

Drawing-book. Crayon.
Ht. 0.19; Wdth. 0.135.

We have taken two striking examples of the artist's experimental work from among a number in the Drawing-books. Cf. the "Ateliers" with composition-figures. 89-95, the double figure of 1942 (Pl. 104), *La Femme au miroir* of 1946 (Pl. 124).

1936   **88**
THE MANDOLIN

Chicago, Leigh Bloch Collection.

Signed at bottom right, dated 36.

1937   **89**
WOMAN WITH MANDOLIN

New York, Museum of Modern Art (Mrs. Simon Guggenheim Fund, 1948).

Ht. 1.64; Wdth. 0.97. Signed at bottom left, dated 37.

Although it belongs to the series of feminine figures in an interior (Pls. 89-95, see text p. 53), this figure with mandolin recalls the theme of the Cubist studies of musicians, 1911-1913 (Pls. 21-26) and that of 1915 (Pl. 35).

1936   **90**
WOMAN AT AN EASEL

U.S.A. Private Collection.

Ht. 0.92; Wdth. 0.73. Signed at bottom right, dated 36.

1937   **91**
WOMAN WITH HAT

Paris, Mme Jacqueline Delubac Collection.

Ht. 0.92; Wdth. 0.92. Signed at bottom right.

1939   **92**
THE PAINTER AND HIS MODEL

Walter P. Chrysler, Jr. Collection.

Ht. 1.30; Wdth 1.75.

1936   **93**
THE WOMAN PAINTER

Chicago, Samuel A. Marx Collection.

Ht. 1.30; Wdth. 1.62. Signed at bottom right, dated 36.

1937   **94**
LE DUO

Paris, Musée National d'Art Moderne.

Ht. 1.30; Wdth. 1.00. Signed at bottom right, dated 37.

1939   **95**
THE STUDIO

New York, Paul Rosenberg Collection.

Ht. 1.30; Wdth. 1.46. Signed at bottom left.

1943   **96**
PITCHER AND SKULL

Signed at bottom left, dated 43.

In these years the artist produced several pictures on the same theme. He also repeats the skull in some composed still lifes. See also *drawing* (Pl. p. 18) and the theme of *Vanity*, p. 52 and 56.

1939   **97**
VANITAS

Property of the artist.

Ht. 0.38; Wdth. 0.55. Signed at bottom left and dated 39.
See text, p. 52 and 56.

1942   98

PITCHER, GLASS AND LEMONS

Ht. 0.35; Wdth. about 0.73.
First appearance of the broken table, cf. *Billiards* (Pl. 117).

1942   99

THE OFFERING

Property of the artist.
Ht. 0.27; Wdth. 0.22.   Engraved plaster with black background.

1939   100

THE GLASS OF WINE

Signed at bottom left, dated 39.

1942   101

THE BLACK FISH

Paris, Musée National d'Art Moderne.
Ht. 0.33; Wdth. 0.55.
A pendant to it of same dimensions and same date is
The Brown Fish (Musée National d'Art Moderne).

1942   102

THE RED TABLE

Ht. 0.92; Wdth. 0.92.

1942   103

NU A LA TOILETTE

Ht. 1.07; Wdth. 0.68.   Signed at top left, dated 42.

1942   104

DOUBLE FIGURE WITH MARINE BACKGROUND

Ht. 0.50; Wdth. 0.49.   Signed at bottom right, dated 42.

1942   105

PATIENCE

Ht. 1.46; Wdth. 1.14.   Signed at bottom left, G. BRAQUE.
See text p. 58.

1942   106

THE BLUE BASIN

New York, Mr. and Mrs. Abner Goldstone Collection.
Ht. 0.60; Wdth. 0.80.
There exists a variant, *The Green Basin* (Private Collection U.S.A.).

1942-43   107

THE COFFEE-MILL

Ht. 0.77; Wdth. 1.05.   Signed at bottom right.
Also called *La Daurade*.
We have pointed out the analogy with the *Icthus* for the
Tabernacle door of the Church at Assy (Pl. p. 75).

1943   108

THE BLUE GUITAR

One may recall that in 1938 the same subject inspired another composition.

1942   109

LA TOILETTE DEVANT LA FENÊTRE

Property of the artist.
Ht. 1.30; Wdth. 0.81.   Signed at bottom right G. BRAQUE.

There exists a very close variant in its composition, *La Toilette Bleue*, with slightly stronger tonality (reproduced in *Braque le Patron*, Pl. 41; dim. 1.45 × 0.95).
The window theme, begun in 1910, in the *Sacré Cœur* (Pl. 24) and repeated in *Nu de dos à la toilette* (Pl. 103) reappears. (See also Pl. 112 and 119).

1942   110

INTERIOR: PALETTE AND FLOWER POT

U.S.A. Private collection.
Ht. 1.45; Wdth. 1.95.   Signed at bottom left, dated 42.
Another painting, a gray carpet with palette and flowers (*The Pot of Flowers*, 1941, 1.00 × 1.00) less complete in composition, a forerunner of this Interior, is reproduced in *Braque le Patron*.

1943-44   111

LE POÊLE

Ht. 1.46; Wdth. 0.89.

1944   112

LE SALON

Paris, Musée National d'Art Moderne.
Ht. 1.27; Wdth. 1.50.   Signed at bottom left.

1943   113

THE GREEN TABLECLOTH

Paris, Musée National d'Art Moderne.
Ht. 0.38; Wdth. 0.55.   Signed at bottom left.
Remarkable for its design, a recumbent X and its background sections of impasto; same solution in *The Terrace* of 1950 (1.13 × 1.46).   Coll. Hänggi, Basel.
There is a variant (0.47 × 0.63), differently centered, the cloth not cut at the bottom by the frame, and the left hand pot replaced by a bouquet, which is reproduced in Hope, (Pl. 146), wrongly supposed to be in the Musée d'Art Moderne. The theme of the *Green Tablecloth* has produced a number of pictures in which the objects of the still life are different and also the background colors in impasto.

1942-43   114

THE KITCHEN

Paris, Jean Paulhan Collection.
Ht. 1.65; Wdth. 0.80.   Signed at bottom left, dated 42.
A vertical composition, with characteristic strips (cf. Pl. 109, 111).

1943   115

SUNFLOWERS

Paris, Mme Jacqueline Delubac Collection.
Ht. 0.55; Wdth. 0.46.   Signed at top right.

1946   116

SUNFLOWERS

New York, Reader's Digest Collection.
Ht. 1.05; Wdth. 1.05. Signed at bottom right and dated 46.

1944-52   117

BILLIARDS

Mexico City, Gelman Collection.
Ht. 1.95; Wdth. 0.97.   Signed at bottom left.
In addition to this vertical version of "Billiards" and that in width at the Musée National d'Art Moderne (1.50 × 1.94), there is a variant (1.45 × 1.95) in the Leigh Bloch Coll., Chicago.
Structure characteristic by its break, which is found earlier in "Two Lemons" (Pl. 98).

1952   **118**

UNDER THE LAMP

Ht. 0.65; Wdth. 0.81.   Signed at bottom right.
The pinks and mustard browns are characteristic.

1945   **119**

LA TOILETTE AUX CARREAUX VERTS

Another example of the enlargement of a still-life by an open window (cf. Pl. 109).

1944   **120**

THE SICKLE

Ht. 0.61; Wdth. 0.50.
There exists a variant of analogous inspiration *The Bundle of Hay* (repr. *Art Sacré* No. 7, 1946).

1944   **121**

THE PUMPKIN

Private Collection.

Ht. 0,615; Wdth. 0.46.   Signed at bottom right, dated 44.
A slip of wood fixed at the top, and two slips at the sides modify the normal format of the canvas.
See text, p. 57.

1952   **122**

THE SUN'S CHARIOT

Zurich, Gustav Zumsteg Collection.

Plaster in relief.   Signed at bottom left.
A new inverted version of Plaster *Io* (Pl. 76).

1952   **123**

DOUBLE STILL LIFE WITH FLOWERS

Ht. 1.00; Wdth. 1.00.   Signed at bottom left.

1946   **124**

LA FEMME AU MIROIR

Paris, Valentine Dudensing Collection.

Ht. 1.16; Wdth. 1.40.   See text p. 61.

1948   **125**

THE CASE

Ht. 0.92; Wdth. 0.92.

1947   **126**

THE CHAIR

Property of the artist.

Ht. 0.61; Wdth. 0.50.
In 1956 Braque repeats this figuration in new paintings on an ochre background.

1952   **127**

BIRD AND ITS NEST

Ht. 0.175; Wdth. 0.195.   *Drawing-book.*
Cf. Pl. p. 13, the canvas of 1955.
On the theme of the bird, etc... see text p. 68.

1949-52   **128**

ATELIER (II)

Paris, Galerie Maeght.

Ht. 1.30; Wdth. 1.62.   Signed at bottom left.
Mr. John Richardson, who has made a special study of the Atelier series, keeping strictly to that of 1949-1955, classes them as follows; (*Burlington Magazine*, June 1955).

Atelier I, 1949 (Coll. J.-P. Guerlin, Paris) (0.92 × 0.73). - *Atelier II*, 1949 (Galerie Maeght) (1.30 × 1.62) (Pl. 128). - *Atelier III*, 1949 (Coll. Mme Sacher, Pratteln) (Pl. 129) (1.30 × 1.955). - *Atelier IV*, 1949 (Coll. Samuel A. Marx, Chicago) (0.74 × 1.30). - *Atelier V*, 1949 (Coll. Hänggi, Basel) (1.44 × 1.75) (Pl. 130). - *Atelier VI*, 1949-1952 (Galerie Maeght) (1.30 × 1.625) (Pl. 131). - *Atelier VII*, 1949-1955, unfinished (1.45 × 1.45) - *Atelier VIII*, 1954-1955 (Coll. Douglas Cooper) (1.30 × 1.95) (Pl. 132).
See text p. 68.

1949   **129**

ATELIER (III)

Switzerland, Private Collection.

Ht. 1.30 Wdth. 1.95.   Signed at bottom left.

1949   **130**

ATELIER (V)

Basel, Coll. Hänggi.

Ht. 1.44; Wdth. 1.75.   Signed at bottom left.

1949-52   **131**

ATELIER (VI)

Paris, Galerie Maeght.

Ht. 1.30; Wdth. 1.625.   Signed at bottom right.
With sitting bird.

1954-55   **132**

ATELIER (VIII)

Argilliers, Douglas Cooper Collection.

Ht. 1.30; Wdth. 1.95.   Signed at bottom left G. BRAQUE.

1952   **133**

SKETCH FOR THE CEILING AT THE LOUVRE

Ht. 0.155; Wdth. 0.20.   Crayon and gouache.
The *drawing-books* are a witness to the importance of Braque's preliminary work for the ceiling, which was commissioned in 1952, for the Room of Etruscan Antique Art (Salle Henri II) in the Louvre Museum. Braque was then at the height of the "bird" period. Inaugurated in the spring of 1953, the ceiling is made up of a central rectangular panel (3.47 × 5.01) and two oval panels (2.84 × 2.13 and 2.72 × 2.11); the central panel consists of two large birds, black ringed with white, and a deep blue sky with patches of thick white impasto.

1955   **134**

ON THE WING

Property of the artist.

Ht. 1.14; Wdth. 1.695.   Signed at bottom right. (Pl. 127).

1949-54   **135**

AJAX

U.S.A. Private Collection.

Ht. 1.80; Wdth. 0.72.   Paper on canvas.
This large figure, a recollection (or contemporary version) of the *Theogony*, is, with the *Canephorae* (Pl. 46) and *Night* (Pl. 136), one of Braque's rare upright figures.

1951   **136**

NIGHT

Ht. 1.625; Wdth. 0.73.
Gray, brown and black tonality.

BIBLIOGRAPHY

In view of the very complete Bibliography by Hannah B. MULLER (Museum of Modern Art, 1948, op. cit,) we are only mentioning here the basic works and the most recent.

Braque's reflections on art, published in fragments in various reviews and albums, as well as in "Braque le Patron" and the "Cahier 1916-1947" (see summary in HOPE op. cit., by Hannah B. MULLER, 12 Nos.) have been continued and completed in the "Le Jour et la Nuit", "Cahiers de Georges Braque, 1917-1952" (16 × 10,5), 2 drawings, 61 pages, Gallimard, Paris, 1952.

Observations in the course of interviews given by him, have been published: in "Cahiers d'Art", No. 10 and in the July 1939 number; in "Lettres Françaises" March 15, 1946; in the revue "Misue", interview with A. IMAIZUMI, in japanese, October 1952; with Dora VALLIER, "Cahiers d'Art", Spring 1954; and with John RICHARDSON, Burlington Magazine, June 1955.

PAULHAN, Jean, Braque le patron.
First edition, de luxe (37×28,5). 225 + x ex., ed. Mourlot, Paris 1945.

Original cover in colored lithograph. With a original lithograph *La Mandoline*, in 8 colors (24,5 × 17). 80 pages with 19 paintings reproduced in colored lithographs by Mourlot frères, introduced in the text.

Other editions:
format 19 × 23, 59 p. 56 helio pl. and 1 col. Ed. Trois Collines, Geneva 1946.

Reprint text of original Mourlot edition, with three new chapters. Jean Paulhan's text was first published in *Poesie* 43, and translated into English in *Horizon* No. 65, pp. 329-339, May 1945. Braque's reflections contained in the book were published in *Open og*, Amsterdam, No. 1, pp. 15-16, September 1946.
format 19 × 14, Gallimard, Paris 1952.

Cahiers de Georges Braque, 1916-1947.

a) First edition, de luxe (50 × 33) 98 pages of manuscript, each with drawing; with a manuscript text by the artist. Original cover in three colors (title, borders, floral ornaments). Mourlot Frères, lithograph. Ed. Maeght, Paris 1948 (October 28, 1947).

b) Second edition, semi-luxe, similar to the former (38.5 × 28) with 1 litho in color. Ed. Maeght, Paris, 1948, Mourlot Frères, lithograph (January 20, 1948).

c) Edition in fac simile, reduced format (31 × 23,5) called *"Cahier de Georges Braque 1917-1947"*. New cover by G. Braque, Ed. Maeght, Paris 1948.

d) Le Jour et la Nuit : Cahiers de Georges Braque 1917-1952 (16×10,5), 61 p., 2 drawings, Gallimard, Paris 1952.

REVERDY. Pierre, Braque: Une aventure méthodique (Nov. 3, 1946). (44 × 32) 250 + xv ex. Ed. Mourlot, Paris 1949.

64 pages of text, 2 original lithographs in color (44 × 37 and 26 × 26) and 27 lithos in black (7,5 × 15,5 roughly) introduced in the text; followed by 10 paintings reproduced in fac-simile in colored lithographs, with an *état de planche* executed by the artist and I painting in indelible ink on paper. Mourlot lithograph.
Pierre Reverdy friend of long standing, accompanies his essay with recollections. Very interesting to consult.

———

APOLLINAIRE, Guillaume, Preface to the catalogue of the Braque Exhibition, Galerie Kahnweiler, November 1908.

VAUXCELLES, Louis, (Georges Braque), *Gil Blas*, March 10, 1908 and November 14, 1908.

APOLLINAIRE, Guillaume, [Georges Braque], *Le Mercure de France*, January 16, 1909.

VAUXCELLES, Louis, [Georges Braque], *Le Télégramme*, January 5, 1909, and *Gil Blas*, March 25, 1909.

APOLLINAIRE, Guillaume, Les Peintres cubistes, pp. 40-42. Figuière, Paris 1913; new ill. ed., Pierre Cailler, Geneva 1950.

Les Soirées de Paris, Special No., August 15, 1914.

LHOTE, André, Braque (Exh. Gal. Léonce Rosenberg) *Nouvelle Revue Française*, No. 69, pp. 153-157, June 1, 1919.

CENDRARS, Blaise, *La Rose rouge*, June 1919.

Cahiers d'Art, Spécial number, Georges Braque, No. 1-2, pp. 1-86, with 163 reproductions, 1933 (format of the review 31,5 × 25).

Texts by Christian Zervos, Jean Cassou, H.S. Ede; and Roger Bissière, André Breton, Blaise Cendrars, Carl Einstein, André Lhote, André Salmon, A. Soffici, taken from earlier publications.
Very important basic publication.

EINSTEIN, Carl, Georges Braque (28,5 × 22,5), 140 p., 96 Pl. in black, 8 col. Ed. Chroniques du Jour, Paris 1934.
The first important monograph published on Braque.

JEDLICKA, Gotthard, Matisse, Picasso, Braque, Oprecht and Helbling, Zurich 1934.

HUYGHE, René, Histoire de l'Art Contemporain: La Peinture, passim, ill., Alcan, Paris 1935.

Reprints articles published by himself and his collaborators in *L'Amour de l'Art*, pp. 209-240, November 1933.

HUYGHE, René, *Les Contemporains*, Tisné, Paris 1939; new ed. 1949, pp. 58-68, 93, 5 pl. of which 1 in color. Eng. Ed. 1939, 4 pl. of which 1 in color.

FUMET, Stanislas, Braque, 14 ill. p. and 24 col. pl., 26.5 × 21, Coll. " Couleurs des Maîtres ", Braun, Paris 1945. English Edition, 1945.

GRENIER, Jean, Braque: Peintures 1909-1947, 8 p. and 16 col. pl., in folio, Ed. du Chêne, Paris 1948; Eng. Ed. with text by Douglas Cooper, Lindsay Drummond, Ltd, London 1948.

PONGE, Francis, Le peintre à l'étude, Gallimard, Paris 1948.

ZAHAR, Marcel, L'orientation de Georges Braque, in: Panorama des Arts, pp. 148-149, ill., portr., Aimery Somogy, Paris 1948.

HOPE, Henry R., Georges Braque, 22,5 × 19, 172 p., bound, col. jacket. The Museum of Modern Art, New York 1949 (in collaboration with the Cleveland Museum of Art).

Published at the time of the large exhibition at the Museum of Modern Art. Preface by Jean CASSOU, pp. 7-9; Georges Braque by Henry R. HOPE, pp. 10-155; work engraved by William S. LIEBERMANN, pp. 156-158; Catalogue of the exhibition; a very important Bibliography, a basic work, by Hannah B. MULLER, 183 nos. The book reproduces 123 paintings, 10 in col., 7 sculptures, 1 drawing, 2 engravings, 4 lithographs and 6 photographs.
A remarkable document.

Life, G. Braque, p. 80-86, May 2, 1949.

At the time of the exhibition at the Museum of Modern Art. Gives 6 portraits of which 1 large col. p., repro. 15 paintings of which 8 in col.

LEJARD, André, Braque, 8 p., 24 col. pl. (18 × 11,5), Bibl. Aldine des Arts, Hazan, Paris 1949.

DEGAND, Léon, Braque (à propos des Ateliers), ill., no. 7-8, *Art d'Aujourd'hui*, 1950.

BOURET, Jean, Braque ou l'andante noir et gris, February 17, 1950, *Arts*.

KAHNWEILER, Daniel H., Les temps héroïques du Cubisme, Braun, Paris 1950.

PONGE, Francis, Braque: Dessins, 16 pl. in black, in quarto, Braun, Paris 1950.

RAYNAL, Maurice (etc...) Histoire de la Peinture moderne, (34,5 × 25,5); II. p. 43, 1 pl. col; III, note p. 120, passim, 9 Col. pl., Skira, Geneva 1950.

CHAR, René, Georges Braque, pp. 141-155, repro. 1 litho. ex., 10 pictures, and 4 col. pl, *Cahiers d'Art*, 1951.

SOLIER, René de, L'œuvre gravée de Braque, *Cahiers de la Pléiade*, XII, 1951.

CHAUDET Henriette, and SEGONZAC, Hubert de, Georges Braque, le « Père Tranquille » du Cubisme, *Paris-Match*, No. 271, June 5, 1952. Reportage: 17 photos of which 6 in color.

GRAND, P.-M., Céramiques de peintres, No. 32, *Art et Décoration*, 1952.

Yomuri, Georges Braque, (published by the newspaper), Tokyo 1952.

A splendid album made even more attractive by the unusual elegance of Japanese typography, published at the time of the Braque exhibition in Tokyo. 34 × 26; 53 col. pl. 38 black, 1 portrait (by Mariette Lachaud), photo of the exhibition's poster. Introduction (in French) by Jean CASSOU; preface by M. Nagasatake ASANO, Director of the Tokyo National Museum, and by Mr. Shoji YASUDA, Director of the newspaper *Yomuri*.

Misue, monthly art review, Tokyo, special number on Braque, No. 566, Octobre 1952.

38 repro. of which 8 col. texts by A. IMAIZUMI, visit to Georges Braque (in Japanese) and Francis PONGE. With two MS. letters of Braque.

STERLING, Charles, La Nature morte de l'Antiquité à nos jours, pp. 96-102 and passim, 1 repro. and 2 col. pl., Tisné, Paris 1952.

P.C., Le Plafond de Braque du Louvre, May 10, 1953, Journal de l'Amateur d'Art.

IMBOURG, Pierre, Braque a pensé plafond, June 10, 1953, No. 113, *Journal de l'Amateur d'Art*.

Le Point, Braque, special number, 48 ill. p., No. 46, Souillac, 1953.

RIBEMONT-DESSAIGNES, Georges, (Braque says: " L'abstrait c'est de la peinture mondaine, un tableau est fini quand il a effacé l'idée ", September 3, 1953, *Arts*.

Verve, vol. VII, No. 27-28, 1953, Specially designed cover, frontispiece, front and back (lithos: bouquet, sitting bird, pp. 76-82, Propos de Braque, 7 col. pl., repro. of 4 pictures, 1 engraved plaster, 3 drawings, 2 photographs by Mariette Lachaud: Views of Varengeville.

SEUPHOR, Michel, L'œuvre graphique de Braque, 22 × 12, 2 p., 19 small repro. of which 10 in col. Printed by Jacomet. Specially designed cover by Georges Braque. Berggruen, Paris 1953.

RAYNAL, Maurice, (texts by), La Peinture moderne, 340 p. (34,5 × 25,5); numerous references to Braque, passim, note p. 295, 12 col. p. (continues and completes 1950 Ed. same Editor.), Skira, Geneva 1953.

BARR, Alfred H. Jr., Masters of Modern Art, p. 95 and 2 col. pl., The Museum of Modern Art, New York, 1954.

LAUFER, Fritz, Braque, in octavo, 30 p., 52 pl. 8 col., Alfred Scherz, Berne 1954.

VALLIER, Dora, Entretien avec Braque: La peinture et nous, propos recueillis, p. 13-14, 1 por., 7 repro., 1 col., Cahiers d'Art, 1954.

France-Illustration, A Varengeville avec Georges Braque No. 417, December 1954. Reportage: 8 p. un-numbered, 9 photos and 3 col.

AULANIER, Christiane, La double origine du plafond de la Salle Henri II au Louvre, pp. 99-104, ill., Revue des Arts. 1954.

Dictionnaire de la Peinture Moderne, note by Frank ELGAR, pp. 35-40, 6 col. repro., Hazan, Paris 1954.

FRANCASTEL, Pierre (in coll. with Galienne FRANCASTEL and Pierre TISNÉ), Histoire de la peinture française, pp. 134-151, 180, 5 pl. of which 1 col. (34,5 × 25), Ed. Elsevier, Brussels and Paris, 1955.

RICHARDSON, John, The "Ateliers" of Braque, Burlington Magazine, No. 627, pp. 162, 164-171, June 1955.

Important. Reproduces and classifies the 8 Ateliers of 1949-1955.

RICHARDSON, John, Le nouvel Atelier de Braque, L'Oeil, No 6, pp. 20-25, June 15, 1955.

Reproduces in color on double page, the Atelier VIII prior to its completion (Coll. Douglas Cooper) and two of the Varengeville windows, with drawings, preliminary gouaches, photographs in the studio, etc... 7 repro., of which 2 in color.

Verve, special number "Les Carnets intimes de Braque" Vol. VIII, Nos. 31-32, in folio, 160 p. 19 pl. in col. 105 pl. in black, Teriade, Paris 1955.

Introduction by Will GROHMANN; L'oreille dans la serrure, by Antoine TUDAL; Les Carnets intimes de Braque, by Rebecca WEST.

Remarkable special number, publishing for the first time, and in large format, sketches (pencil, Indian ink, wash, gouache colors) of the Carnets intimes. Technical execution of an exceptional quality, by Mourlot and Draeger.

The XXᵉ Siècle, Une quête de Cubisme, Le papier collé, by Frank Elgar, No. 6, January 1956.
7 works of Braque repro. amongst which Aria de Bach, Tivoli Cinema.

GIEURE, Maurice, Georges Braque, Dessins, (18.5 × 13) bound, 3 p., 80 pl. in black, Ed. des Deux-Mondes, Paris 1956. (Includes lithos and engraved plasters).

VERDEL, André, Georges Braque, 36 p. with 20 photographs, by Roger HAUERT, and 3 drawings, in octavo, "Les grands Peintres", Ed. René Kister, Geneva, 1956.

EXHIBITIONS

1906 - SALON DES INDÉPENDANTS, Paris (7 Exh.).

1907 - SALON D'AUTOMNE, Paris (1 Exh.).
 - SALON DES INDÉPENDANTS, Paris (6 Exh.).

1908 - November 9-28, Galerie Kahnweiler, Paris (27 Exh.).
 Catalogue with preface by Guillaume APOLINAIRE.

1909 - SALON DES INDÉPENDANTS, Paris (2 Exh.).

1913 - February-May, Armory Show (Association of American Painters and Sculptors), New York, Chicago, Boston (3 Exh.).
 First exhibition in the United States.

1914 - Galerie Emil Richter, Dresden (38 Exh.); same exhibition at the Feldmann Gallery, Berlin.

1914 - December 9-January 9 1915, Photo Secession Gallery, New York (38 Exh.).—With Picasso.

1919 - March 5-31, Galerie Léonce Rosenberg, Paris.

1920 - SALON D'AUTOMNE, Paris (3 Exh.).
 - SALON DES INDÉPENDANTS, Paris (4 Exh.).

1921 - May 30, Uhde Auction, Hôtel Drouot, Paris (17 Exh.).
 - June 13-14, Kahnweiler Auction, First part, Hôtel Drouot, Paris (22 Exh.).
 - November 17-18, Kahnweiler Auction, Second part, Hôtel Drouot, Paris (38 Exh.).

1922 - July 4, Kahnweiler Auction, Third part, Hôtel Drouot, Paris (18 Exh.).
 - SALON D'AUTOMNE, Paris (18 Exh.).

1923 - May 7, Kahnweiler Auction, Fourth part, Hôtel Drouot, Paris (85 Exh.).

1924 - May 2-21, Galerie Paul Rosenberg, Paris (16 Exh.).

1925 - March, Flechtheim Gallery, Berlin.

1926 - March 8-27, Galerie Paul Rosenberg, Paris (62 Exh.).

1930 - May, Galerie Paul Rosenberg, Paris (62 Exh.).
 - September 21, MATISSE, BRAQUE, PICASSO, October 15, Flechtheim Gallery, Berlin (24 Exh. Braque).

1933 - April 9-May 14, BRAQUE, Kunsthalle, Basel (193 Exb. of which 3 papiers collés, 2 sanguines, 2 drawings, 4 plasters).
 Cat. with intr. by Carl EINSTEIN; 38 repro.
 The most important exhibition consecrated to Braque.
 The Cahiers d'Art published at this time a Braque album (163 repro.); see bibliography.

1934 - March 13-31, BRAQUE, MATISSE, PICASSO, Durand-Ruel Gallery, New York, (13 Exh.).
 - July, Alex Reid and Lefevre Galleries, London (41 Exh).
 - November 26-December 15, ŒUVRES RÉCENTES, Valentine Gallery, New York (16 Exh.).

1935 - March-April, *LES CREATEURS DU CUBISME*, Galerie des Beaux Arts, Paris (25 Exh.).

  Catalogue with preface by Maurice RAYNAL; text by Raymond COGNIAT.

1936 - January 8-31, *ŒUVRES RÉCENTES*, Galerie Paul Rosenberg, Paris (20 Exh.).

  - July, Alex Reid and Lefevre Galleries, London (41 Exh).

  - March 2-April 19, *CUBISM AND ABSTRACT ART*, Museum of Modern Art, New York, (9 Exh. Braque).

  - November-December, Palais des Beaux-Arts, Brussels (81 Exh.).

  - The 1936 International Exhibition of Paintings, Pittsburgh, Carnegie Institute.
  Braque is awarded the first price for *"The Yellow Tablecloth"*.

1937 - January 6-30, *MATISSE, BRAQUE, PICASSO*, Galerie Paul Rosenberg, Paris (20 Exh. Braque).

  - April 3-30, *ŒUVRES RÉCENTES*, Galerie Paul Rosenberg, Paris (18 Exh.).

  - June-October, *MAITRES DE L'ART INDÉPENDANT (1895-1937)*, Musée Municipal d'Art Moderne (Petit Palais), Paris (25 Exh. Braque).

1938 - February, 4-21, *L'ÉPOQUE FAUVE DE BRAQUE*, 1906, Galerie Pierre.

1938 - July, Paul Rosenberg and Helft Galleries, Ltd, London (22 Exh.).

  - October 14-25, Buchholz Gallery, New York (16 Exh.),

  - November 16-December 10, Galerie Paul Rosenberg. Paris (22 Exh.).

  - *MATISSE, PICASSO, BRAQUE, LAURENS*, Stockholm, Oslo, Copenhagen and Gothenburg (39 Exh. Braque).

  Catalogue with text by Walther HALVORSEN.

1939 - April 4-29, Galerie Paul Rosenberg (27 Exh.).

  - June 6-July 8, *ŒUVRES RÉCENTES*, Rosenberg and Helft Galleries, London, (24 Exh.).

  - November 7-27, *RETROSPECTIVE*, Arts Club of Chicago (68 Exh.).

  Catalogue with preface by Henry McBRIDE; introduction by Hames Johnson SWEENEY.

  - December 6-Juanary 6, 1940, *RETROSPECTIVE* (part of the former, 55 Exh). Duncan Phillips Memorial Gallery, Washington.

  Catalogue with texts by Duncan PHILLIPS Henry McBRIDE and James Johnson SWEENEY.

1940 - February 6-March 3, *RETROSPECTIVE* (see two earlier ones), Museum of Art, San Francisco (67 Exh.).

  - *A.E. GALLATIN COLLECTION*, New York (11 Exh. Braque). Subsequently at the Philadelphia Museum.

  Critical notes by Georges L.K. MORRIS, Introduction by Jean HELION.

1941 - February 6-March 4, *CHRYSLER COLLECTION*, Virginia Museum of Fine Arts, Richmond, U.S. (15 Exh.). Same exhibition at Philadelphia.

  - January 13-February 8, Valentine Gallery, New York (27 Exh.).

1942 - April 7-25, Galerie Paul Rosenberg, New York (13 Exh.).

  - November 22-December 27, Museum of Art, Baltimore (16 Exh.).

1943 - April 6-May 1, *BRAQUE AND PICASSO* (6 Exh.). Galerie Paul Rosenberg, New York.

  - September 25-October 31, *SALON D'AUTOMNE*, Paris (35 Exh.) 26 paintings, 9 sculptures.

1944 - October 6-November 5, *SALON D'AUTOMNE*, Paris (2 Exh.).

1945 - April 15-May 15, *LES EMAUX DE LIGUGÉ*, Galerie de France, 32 Exh., 8 of Braque (ewers, round plates in enameled copper).

  - May 24-June 30, *LE CUBISME*, 1911-1918, Galerie de France, 9 Exh. of Braque.

  Catalogue 59 p.; preface by Bernard DORIVAL; bibliographical note; note on *La Guitare* (1915) by André LHOTE.

  - June-November, *BRAQUE, PICASSO, LÉGER*, Museum of Art, Philadelphia (9 Exh.).

  - October 20-November 12, Stedelijk Museum, Amsterdam (26 Exh.).

  - November 24-December 13, Palais des Beaux-Arts, Brussels (27 Exh.). Continuation of the former.

1946 - April, *EXPOSITION D'ART SACRÉ*, Galerie René Drouin (with Rouault) (1 Braque, *Vanitas*).

  Catalogue with preface by the Abbé MOREL (repro. *Vanitas*).

  - April 29-May 18, Paul Rosenberg Gallery, New York (11 Exh.).

  - May, *BRAQUE, ROUAULT*, Tate Gallery, London (28 Nos. Braque).

  - Catalogue with introduction by Germain BAZIN; 6 repr.; front cover by Braque, in 2 col.

  - June 28-september 30 , *BRAQUE, PICASSO*, Art Institute, Chicago (5 Exh).

  - September 21-October 20, *BRAQUE, KANDINSKY, PICASSO*, Kunsthaus, Zurich (26 Exh.). Continuation of the Tate Gallery exhibition.

1947 - June, Galerie Maeght, Paris (58 Exh.).
  Cover of cat. with colored litho; 5 repro. in black; texts by René CHAR, Georges BRAQUE, Jacques KOBER.

  - June 27-September 30, *PEINTURES ET SCULPTURES CONTEMPORAINES*, Palais des Papes, Avignon (13 Exh.).

1948 - January 5-24, Paul Rosenberg Gallery, New York (15 Exh.).

  - February 26-March 24, *BRAQUE, PICASSO, GRIS*, Kunsthalle, Basel, (40 Exh.).

  - April 2-29, Kunsthalle, Berne (37 Exh.). Continuation of the former.

  - May-October, *EXH. BIENNALE*, Venise (18 Exh.).
  Braque is awarded the Grand Prix of the Biennale for *"Billiard"*.

1949 - Spring, Museum of Modern Art, New York (115 Exh.), 85 pictures, 5 drawings, 14 engravings and illustr.; 11 sculptures.

The most important exhibition in America. The Museum of Modern Art publish at this time the book by Henry R. HOPE (see *biblio.*).

- The same exhibition at Cleveland; cat. with introduction by Jean CASSOU.

- Stuttgart, *GEORGES BRAQUE: GEMAELDE, GRAPHIK, PLASTIK*; with the collaboration of the military government at Baden.

1950 - April 29-May 29, *LES FAUVES*, Berne, Kunsthalle, 143 Exh. (11 Braque; 1 repro. col., 1 black in cat.).

- September, *BRAQUE*, Galerie Samlaren. Stockholm 56 Exh, of which 14 in oil).

- *GEORGES BRAQUE: DAS GRAPHISCHE WERK*, Buchheim, Feldafing, Germany. Text by Lothar-Gunther BUCHHEIM. With catalogue essay of engraved work 1912-1950. 14 repro. and a portrait.

1951 - *SUR QUATRE MURS*. (Braque shows 3 engraved and colored plasters.) Galerie Maeght, Paris.

Cat. with text by Pierre REVERDY, ornamented with small original lithographs by Georges Braque.

- June-September, *LE FAUVISME*, Paris, Musée National d'Art Moderne (141 Exh. 11 Braque, 2 repro. in cat.).

1952 - April-September, *LA NATURE MORTE DE L'AN-TIQUITÉ A NOS JOURS*, (2 Exh. Braque: *The Black Rose, The Pink Tablecloth*), Catalogue by Charles STERLING. Musée de l'Orangerie, Paris.

- June-July, *GEORGES BRAQUE*, 41 Exh. (6 lithos in color), Galerie Maeght, Paris.
Catalogue with texts by Alberto GIACOMETTI and Jean GRENIER.

- March-April, *CINQUANTE ANS DE PEINTURE FRANÇAISE DANS LES COLLECTIONS PAR-TICULIÈRES: DE CÉZANNE A MATISSE*, Paris, Musée des Arts Décoratifs (201 Exh; 7 Braque; 2 repro. in cat.).

- *BRAQUE* Exhibition, Tokyo, Japan.

We have this information from the specialnumber; of the review "*Misue*", No. 566. October 1952. 38 repro. in black, 8 col. cover in color. Text by Francis PONGE (in French), "L'Art de Georges Braque"; in Japanese; "Visit to Georges Braque" by A. IMAIZUMI.

- May-June, *L'ŒUVRE DU XXᵉ SIÈCLE*, Paris, Musée National d'Art Moderne. (114 Exh. paintings; 5 Braque, 1 repro. in cat.).

1953 - January 30-April 9, *LE CUBISME*, 1907-1914 (231 Exh. 24 Braque), Musée National d'Art Moderne, Paris.

Cat. with introduction by Jean CASSOU; chronological table by Bernard DORIVAL; cat. with the assistance of Madame Gabrielle VIENNE (6 Braque repro.).

- Avril-25 May 31, *BRAQUE*, Berne, Kunsthalle. 157 Exh. (114 canvases, 3 drawings, 28 engravings, 1 tapestry, 11 sculptures); Same exhibition at Zurich.

Preface to cat. by A. RUDLINGER, Repro. 1 portrait, 19 pictures.

Very important.

- November 14-December 6, *L'ŒUVRE GRAPHIQUE DE BRAQUE*, Musée des Beaux-Arts, Liège (96 Exh.). Catalogue and text by Michel SEUPHOR.

- November 20 - December 15, *SCULTURE BY PAINTERS*, Curt Valentine gallery (ex Buchholz), New-York. (76 Exh., 6 Braque).

1954 - May 14-July 3, *BRAQUE, PAINTINGS AND DRAWINGS FROM COLL. IN ENGLAND, WITH LITHOGRAPHS*, 1909-1953, ICA Gallery, London.

- December-January 1955, *LA THEOGONIE D'HE-SIODE ET DE BRAQUE*, with sculptures and engraved plasters by Braque, of Greek inspiration. Galerie Maeght, Paris.

Cat. 32 × 28 with preface by Georges LIMBOUR: 9 repro. in phototype of preparatory drawings and a fac-simile.

- *DESSINS: DE TOULOUSE LAUTREC AUX CUBISTES*, (246 Exh. 9 Braque). Cat. by Bernard DORIVAL; Musée d'Art Moderne, Paris.

1955 - January-July, *BRAQUE, DAS GRAPHISCHE GE-SAMTWORK*, 1907-1955, Cologne, Bremen, Dusseldorf, Krefeld, Berlin. 59 Exh. and 10 illustrated books.

Catalogue 32 × 23,5. Cover 2 col; 4 large repro. in black; one litho in color, double page size, life-size. Preface by Paul WEMBER.

Contains small black repro. of the 59 Exh. (methodical catalogue of great use) and also 24 repro. of the book illustrations.

- May 31-September 5, *PAINTINGS FROM PRI-VATE COLLECTIONS*, (25th *anniversary*), The Museum of Modern Art, New York (5 Exh.).

1956 - February-April, *THE HERMANN RUPF COLLEC-TION*, Kunstmuseum, Berne (10 Exh. Braque) 9 repro. in cat.

May-June, *TOILES RÉCENTES DE GEORGES BRAQUE*, Galerie Maeght. Paris.

TABLE OF CONTENTS